SIMPLE ECONOMICS

FOR COMPETITIVE EXAMS

RAYEES ALI

Dear readers,

I would like to dedicate this book to my parents, and Aman. They have been my constant source of inspiration and support throughout my life. Their unwavering love and guidance have helped me become the person I am today.

My parents have always encouraged me to pursue my dreams and have instilled in me the values of hard work, determination, and perseverance. They have taught me to never give up on my goals, no matter how difficult they may seem.

I am grateful for their sacrifices and the many opportunities they have provided me with. They have always been there to cheer me on, to celebrate my achievements, and to pick me up when I fall.

To my parents, I want to say thank you for everything you have done for me. This book is a testament to your love and support, and I hope it makes you proud.

With love and gratitude,

RAYEES ALI

Contents

Foreword

Rayees Ali is a well-known author, educator, vlogger, and content creator who has made a significant impact in the world of education and personal development. With over a decade of experience in teaching and learning, Rayees has become a trusted authority on a range of subjects, including economics, business, finance, and personal growth.

As an author, Rayees has written several books that aim to simplify complex concepts and make them accessible to a wider audience. His writing style is engaging and easy to understand, making his books popular among students, professionals, and enthusiasts alike. He has authored books on various topics, including economics, entrepreneurship, investing, and personal finance.

As an educator, Rayees has a passion for teaching and sharing knowledge with others. He has taught in various academic institutions and has also developed online courses that have helped thousands of learners worldwide. He believes in the power of education to transform lives and help individuals reach their full potential.

As a vlogger and content creator, Rayees has a strong online presence, with a large following on social media platforms such as YouTube and Instagram. He uses these platforms to share his knowledge and expertise with a wider audience, and his videos and posts are informative, engaging, and often thought-provoking.

Rayees is also a strong advocate for personal growth and development, and he believes that anyone can achieve success with the right mindset and approach. He often shares his insights and tips for personal growth and success, helping individuals to develop their skills, improve their mindset, and achieve their goals.

In conclusion, Rayees Ali is a multi-talented individual who has made a significant impact in the worlds of education and personal development. His books, teaching, and online content have helped countless individuals to learn, grow, and achieve their goals. With his passion for knowledge and his commitment to making learning accessible to all, Rayees is an inspiration to many and a valuable resource for anyone looking to expand their knowledge and skills.

I dedicate my work to my parents and Aman with deep gratitude and love. My parents have been a constant source of support and inspiration throughout my life. They have always encouraged me to pursue my dreams and have provided me with the tools and opportunities to succeed. Their unwavering love and belief in me have been instrumental in shaping who I am today.I also dedicate this work to Aman, who has been a close friend and mentor. Aman's guidance and support have been invaluable to me throughout my academic and professional journey. His unwavering commitment to excellence and his dedication to helping others have inspired me to strive for the same. I am deeply grateful to my parents and Aman for their unwavering love, support, and guidance. Their presence in my life has made all the difference, and I am honored to dedicate this work to them.

Acknowledgements

Writing a book is a long and challenging process, and it would not have been possible without the support and encouragement of many people. I would like to express my deepest gratitude to all those who have helped me along the way.

First and foremost, I would like to thank my family for their unwavering support and encouragement. Their love and encouragement kept me going even during the most difficult moments of this journey. I am grateful for the sacrifices they have made to help me pursue my passion for economics.

I would like to extend my heartfelt thanks to my colleagues, mentors, and friends who have provided valuable feedback, suggestions, and support throughout this process. Your insights and suggestions have helped me shape this book and make it the best it can be.

I would also like to thank the team at the publishing house for their hard work and dedication in bringing this book to life. Their expertise and guidance have been invaluable in shaping the final product.

Last but not least, I would like to express my gratitude to all the readers who have taken the time to read this book. Your interest and support mean the world to me, and I hope that this book has helped you in some way to better understand the fascinating world of economics.

Thank you all for being a part of this journey.
Sincerely,
RAYEES ALI
reach me : rayeesalinajar222@gmail.com

Prologue

Economics is the study of how individuals, businesses, governments, and societies allocate their resources to meet their needs and wants. It is a social science that seeks to explain and understand the behavior of markets, the role of government, and the interactions between different economic agents.

As an economist, I have always been fascinated by the complex interplay of economic forces that shape our world. From the decisions of individuals to the policies of governments, economics provides a lens through which we can analyze and understand the workings of our society.

In this book, I aim to provide a comprehensive introduction to the field of economics, covering everything from basic concepts and theories to real-world applications and current debates. I hope to demystify economics and make it accessible to readers from all backgrounds, whether you are a student, a professional, or simply interested in understanding how our economy works.

Through a combination of clear explanations, real-world examples, and thought-provoking insights, I hope to take you on a journey through the fascinating world of economics. Whether you are interested in understanding the forces that drive economic growth, the impact of globalization on our society, or the role of government in regulating markets, this book has something for you.

So, join me as we explore the exciting and ever-evolving world of economics. I promise you, it will be a journey you will not forget.

Introduction to Economics

Chapter 1: Introduction to Economics This chapter will introduce the basic principles of economics, including the study of scarcity, opportunity cost, and the economic problem. It will also cover the types of economies, including command, market, and mixed economies.

Economics is a social science that studies how individuals, businesses, governments, and societies allocate limited resources to satisfy their unlimited wants and needs. It is concerned with the production, distribution, and consumption of goods and services, and how individuals and groups make decisions about these economic activities.

At its core, economics is about choice and trade-offs. Resources such as time, money, and labor are scarce, and we must make choices about how to allocate them. For example, if a person decides to spend money on a new smartphone, they are choosing to forego spending that money on something else, such as a new computer or vacation.

Economics is divided into two main branches: microeconomics and macroeconomics. Microeconomics focuses on individual economic units, such as households, firms, and markets. It explores how these units interact and make decisions about the production and consumption of goods and services. Macroeconomics, on the other hand, examines the economy as a whole, including issues such as inflation, unemployment, and economic growth.

Economics also has many practical applications. It helps us understand the behavior of markets and how to make informed decisions about investments, business operations, and public policy. For example, economic principles can help businesses decide on pricing strategies, governments develop policies to promote economic growth and stability, and individuals make informed decisions about their personal finances.

In summary, economics is a social science that studies how individuals and societies make choices about the allocation of limited resources to satisfy their unlimited wants and needs. It is a practical discipline with applications in many areas of life and provides insights into the workings of markets and economies.

1. Adam Smith: "The wealth of a nation consists not in the abundance of its treasures, but in the annual produce of its land and labour."
2. Alfred Marshall: "Economics is a study of mankind in the ordinary business of life."
3. Lionel Robbins: "Economics is the science which studies human behaviour as a relationship between ends and scarce means which have alternative uses."
4. Paul Samuelson: "Economics is the study of how people and society end up choosing, with or without the use of money, to employ scarce productive resources that could have alternative uses, to produce various commodities and distribute them for consumption, now or in the future, among various persons and groups in society."
5. Milton Friedman: "Economics is a science of human action, that is, a study of how men and women respond to incentives and how those responses, in turn, affect human behavior."
6. Amartya Sen: "Economics is concerned with the living conditions of people, and the decisions they make in order to improve those conditions."
7. John Maynard Keynes: "The study of economics does not seem to require any specialized gifts of an unusually high order. Is it not, intellectually regarded, a very easy subject compared with the higher branches of philosophy and pure science?"

These definitions highlight the different approaches and perspectives in economics, from a focus on wealth and production to the study of human behavior and decision-making.

There are four main types of economies:

1. Traditional economy: In a traditional economy, economic decisions are based on traditions, customs, and beliefs that have been passed down through generations. This type of economy is often found in rural, undeveloped areas where people live off the land and engage in

subsistence farming or hunting and gathering. Traditional economies are often characterized by a lack of technological innovation and limited trade with other economies.

2. Market economy: In a market economy, economic decisions are made by individuals and firms who interact through markets. Prices and supply and demand determine what goods and services are produced and consumed. The role of government in a market economy is limited, and individuals are free to pursue their own self-interest. The United States is an example of a market economy.

3. Command economy: In a command economy, economic decisions are made by a central authority, such as a government or a planning committee. The central authority decides what goods and services are produced, how they are produced, and how they are distributed. The former Soviet Union and Cuba are examples of command economies.

4. Mixed economy: In a mixed economy, economic decisions are made by a combination of individuals, firms, and government. The government plays a significant role in areas such as regulating markets, providing public goods and services, and redistributing income. Most modern economies, including the United States and China, are mixed economies.

It is important to note that economies can vary along a spectrum between these four types. For example, some market economies may have government regulations to protect consumers or promote competition, while some command economies may allow some market activity or private ownership.

Opportunity cost is the cost of choosing one alternative over another. It is the value of the next best alternative that is foregone in order to pursue the chosen option. In other words, opportunity cost is what you give up in order to do or have something else.

For example, if you have $10 and you choose to spend it on a movie ticket, your opportunity cost is what you could have done with that $10 instead, such as buying a book or going out for dinner. The opportunity cost of going to the movie is the value of the next best alternative foregone, such as buying the book or having dinner.

Opportunity cost is an important concept in economics because it helps individuals and businesses make decisions about how to allocate their resources, such as time and money. By considering the opportunity cost of each alternative, they can determine which option will provide the greatest benefit or value.

Opportunity cost is also relevant to trade-offs between different options. When faced with a choice between two or more alternatives, the option with the lower opportunity cost is generally the better choice, since it represents the most efficient use of resources.

Overall, opportunity cost is an essential concept in economics that helps individuals and businesses make informed decisions about how to allocate their resources and maximize their benefits.

1. Which of the following is not a central problem of economics?

   a) What to produce
   b) How to produce
   c) When to produce
   d) For whom to produce

1. Economics is the study of:

   a) Money
   b) Business
   c) Human behaviour
   d) All of the above

3. Which of the following is an example of a scarce resource?

   a) Water
   b) Sunlight
   c) Air
   d) None of the above

4. Which of the following is a factor of production?

   a) Land
   b) Money
   c) Labour
   d) All of the above

5. Which of the following is an example of a market economy?

a) China
b) India
c) United States
d) None of the above

6. Which of the following is not a type of economy?

   a) Traditional economy
   b) Command economy
   c) Global economy
   d) Mixed economy

7. Opportunity cost is:

   a) The cost of production
   b) The cost of choosing one alternative over another
   c) The cost of advertising
   d) The cost of transportation

8. The law of supply states that:

   a) As the price of a good increases, the quantity supplied increase
   b) As the price of a good decreases, the quantity supplied decreases
   c) As the price of a good increases, the quantity supplied decreases
   d) As the price of a good decreases, the quantity supplied increases

9. The law of demand states that:

   a) As the price of a good increases, the quantity demanded increases
   b) As the price of a good decreases, the quantity demanded decreases
   c) As the price of a good increases, the quantity demanded decreases
   d) As the price of a good decreases, the quantity demanded increases

10. Which of the following is not a determinant of demand?

   a) Income
   b) Price of substitutes
   c) Price of the good itself

d) Cost of production

11. Which of the following is not a determinant of supply?

a) Price of the good itself
b) Price of inputs
c) Technology
d) Income

12. A surplus occurs when:

a) Quantity demanded is greater than quantity supplied
b) Quantity supplied is greater than quantity demanded
c) Quantity demanded and quantity supplied are equal
d) None of the above

13. A shortage occurs when:

a) Quantity demanded is greater than quantity supplied
b) Quantity supplied is greater than quantity demanded
c) Quantity demanded and quantity supplied are equal
d) None of the above

14. Which of the following is an example of a public good?

a) Food
b) Clothing
c) National defense
d) Housing

15. Which of the following is an example of a positive externality?

a) Pollution
b) Education
c) Traffic congestion
d) Crime

16. Which of the following is an example of a negative externality?

a) Education
b) Pollution
c) Public parks
d) Healthcare

CHAPTER TWO

Microeconomics

Microeconomics This chapter will cover the principles of microeconomics, including demand and supply, elasticity, production, costs, market structures, and perfect competition.

In economics, demand refers to the willingness and ability of consumers to purchase a particular good or service at a certain price and time. It represents the relationship between the price of a product and the quantity that consumers are willing to buy at that price, given their income and preferences.

The law of demand states that as the price of a good increases, the quantity demanded decreases, and as the price of a good decreases, the quantity demanded increases, ceteris paribus (all other things being equal). This inverse relationship between price and quantity demanded is represented by a downward-sloping demand curve.

The determinants of demand include income, price of related goods (such as substitutes and complements), tastes and preferences, population and demographics, and expected future prices. For example, if the price of a substitute good increases, the demand for the original good may increase as consumers switch to the cheaper option.

Demand is a key concept in economics as it helps businesses determine the price and quantity of goods and services to produce and sell in the market. By understanding consumer demand, businesses can optimize their production and pricing strategies to maximize profits.

In addition, demand is also relevant to public policy, such as taxation and subsidies. For example, if the government increases the tax on cigarettes, the demand for cigarettes may decrease as consumers switch to other products, leading to a decrease in smoking and improved public health outcomes.

In economics, a demand function is a mathematical representation of the relationship between the quantity demanded of a good or service and its various determinants. It is typically expressed as an equation that shows the quantity demanded as a function of the price of the good, income, and other factors that affect demand.

The most basic form of a demand function is:

$Qd = f(P)$

where Qd is the quantity demanded of the good or service and P is its price. This implies that the quantity demanded depends solely on the price of the good or service, holding all other factors constant.

However, demand functions can also include other variables that affect demand, such as income, the prices of related goods, consumer preferences, and demographic factors. For example, a more complex demand function for a specific product might be:

$Qd = f(P, Y, Pr, T, Ps)$

where Y represents income, Pr is the price of related goods (such as substitutes or complements), T is consumer tastes and preferences, and Ps is the size of the population.

The coefficients or parameters of a demand function indicate how changes in the determinants of demand affect the quantity demanded. For instance, if the coefficient of income is positive, it implies that an increase in income will lead to an increase in the quantity demanded of the good or service, all other factors being equal.

Demand functions are useful tools for businesses and policymakers to understand how changes in prices and other determinants of demand affect the quantity demanded of a good or service. They can be used to forecast sales and revenue, optimize pricing strategies, and assess the impact of public policies on consumer behavior.

In economics, a demand curve is a graphical representation of the relationship between the price of a good or service and the quantity demanded of it, holding all other determinants of demand constant. It is a fundamental tool used to analyze the behavior of consumers and businesses in a market economy.

The demand curve is usually plotted with price on the vertical axis and quantity demanded on the horizontal axis. The curve slopes downward from left to right, indicating that as the price of a good or service increases, the quantity demanded decreases, and as the price decreases, the quantity demanded increases.

The shape of the demand curve reflects the law of demand, which states that, ceteris paribus (all other things being equal), as the price of a good or service increases, the quantity demanded of it decreases, and vice versa.

The slope of the demand curve indicates the degree of responsiveness of the quantity demanded to changes in price, known as price elasticity of demand. A steeper demand curve (with a higher absolute value of slope) indicates a more elastic demand, meaning that consumers are more responsive to changes in price. A flatter demand curve (with a lower absolute value of slope) indicates a more inelastic demand, meaning that consumers are less responsive to changes in price.

The position of the demand curve can also shift due to changes in the determinants of demand, such as income, the prices of related goods, consumer preferences, and demographic factors. For example, an increase in income will shift the demand curve for normal goods to the right, while a decrease in income will shift the demand curve to the left.

Demand curves are important for businesses and policymakers to understand the behavior of consumers and how they respond to changes in prices and other determinants of demand. They can be used to estimate the impact of price changes on revenue and profits, to forecast demand and plan production, and to design effective policies to regulate markets.

This demand schedule shows the quantity demanded of a hypothetical good at various prices. As the price of the good increases from $5 to $14, the quantity demanded decreases from 100 units to 10 units. This inverse relationship between price and quantity demanded is represented graphically by a downward-sloping demand curve.

Elasticity of demand is a measure of how responsive the quantity demanded of a good or service is to changes in its price. It measures the percentage change in quantity demanded in response to a 1% change in the price of the good or service, all other things being equal.

The formula for price elasticity of demand is:

Price Elasticity of Demand = % Change in Quantity Demanded / % Change in Price

There are three types of price elasticity of demand:

1. Elastic demand: If the price elasticity of demand is greater than 1, it means that the quantity demanded is very responsive to changes in price. This indicates that consumers are very sensitive to price changes, and small changes in price can cause a large change in the quantity

demanded. Examples of goods with elastic demand include luxury items, such as expensive cars or high-end jewelry.

2. Inelastic demand: If the price elasticity of demand is less than 1, it means that the quantity demanded is not very responsive to changes in price. This indicates that consumers are not very sensitive to price changes, and large changes in price may only cause a small change in the quantity demanded. Examples of goods with inelastic demand include necessities, such as food, gasoline, and medication.

3. Unit elastic demand: If the price elasticity of demand is equal to 1, it means that the quantity demanded is exactly proportional to changes in price. This indicates that consumers are equally sensitive to price changes, and a 1% change in price will cause a 1% change in quantity demanded. Examples of goods with unit elastic demand include many consumer goods, such as clothing and electronics.

Price elasticity of demand is an important concept in economics, as it helps businesses and policymakers understand how changes in price will affect the quantity of a good or service that consumers are willing and able to purchase.

1. Gasoline: If the price of gasoline increases by 10%, and the quantity demanded decreases by 5%, the price elasticity of demand would be:

Price Elasticity of Demand = % Change in Quantity Demanded / % Change in Price Price Elasticity of Demand = (-5%) / (10%) = -0.5
This means that gasoline has an inelastic demand, since the absolute value of the elasticity is less than 1.

1. Chocolate bars: If the price of a chocolate bar decreases by 15%, and the quantity demanded increases by 20%, the price elasticity of demand would be:

Price Elasticity of Demand = % Change in Quantity Demanded / % Change in Price Price Elasticity of Demand = (20%) / (-15%) = -1.33
This means that chocolate bars have an elastic demand, since the absolute value of the elasticity is greater than 1.

3. Pizza: If the price of a large pizza increases by 5%, and the quantity demanded decreases by 5%, the price elasticity of demand would be:

Price Elasticity of Demand = % Change in Quantity Demanded / % Change in Price Price Elasticity of Demand = (-5%) / (5%) = -1
This means that pizza has an elastic demand, since the absolute value of the elasticity is greater than 1.

4. Luxury watches: If the price of a luxury watch increases by 20%, and the quantity demanded decreases by 25%, the price elasticity of demand would be:

Price Elasticity of Demand = % Change in Quantity Demanded / % Change in Price Price Elasticity of Demand = (-25%) / (20%) = -1.25
This means that luxury watches have an elastic demand, since the absolute value of the elasticity is greater than 1.

5. Prescription drugs: If the price of a prescription drug increases by 5%, and the quantity demanded decreases by 2%, the price elasticity of demand would be:

Price Elasticity of Demand = % Change in Quantity Demanded / % Change in Price Price Elasticity of Demand = (-2%) / (5%) = -0.4
This means that prescription drugs have an inelastic demand, since the absolute value of the elasticity is less than 1.

In economics, supply refers to the quantity of a good or service that producers are willing and able to offer for sale at different prices, over a given time period.

The law of supply states that as the price of a good or service increases, the quantity supplied also increases, holding all other factors constant. This relationship is illustrated by the upward-sloping supply curve.

The factors that affect supply include:

1. Price of inputs: The cost of the resources used to produce a good or service, such as labor, raw materials, and energy, affects the supply of the good or service. If the cost of inputs increases, the supply curve shifts leftward, indicating a decrease in supply. If the cost of inputs decreases, the supply curve shifts rightward, indicating an increase in supply.

2. Technology: Improvements in technology can lower the cost of production, which increases the supply of a good or service. For example, advances in farming technology can increase crop yields, which increases the supply of agricultural products.
3. Number of producers: The number of producers in a market affects the supply of a good or service. An increase in the number of producers results in an increase in supply, while a decrease in the number of producers results in a decrease in supply.
4. Expectations of future prices: If producers expect the price of a good or service to increase in the future, they may decrease the current supply in order to sell at a higher price in the future.
5. Government policies: Government policies, such as taxes, subsidies, and regulations, can affect the supply of a good or service. For example, a subsidy for renewable energy production may increase the supply of renewable energy.

Understanding supply is important for businesses and policymakers in making decisions related to production, pricing, and regulation. The interaction of supply and demand in a market determines the equilibrium price and quantity of a good or service.

This supply schedule shows the quantities of widgets that producers are willing and able to supply at different prices. As the price of widgets increases, the quantity supplied also increases, according to the law of supply. For example, at a price of $1 per widget, producers are willing and able to supply 100 widgets, while at a price of $5 per widget, they are willing and able to supply 500 widgets. This relationship is represented graphically by an upward-sloping supply curve.

Bottom of Form

In economics, a supply curve is a graphical representation of the relationship between the price of a good or service and the quantity of that good or service that producers are willing and able to offer for sale at different prices, over a given time period.

The law of supply states that as the price of a good or service increases, the quantity supplied also increases, holding all other factors constant. Therefore, the supply curve is upward-sloping, indicating that as price increases, the quantity supplied increases.

The supply curve is typically drawn as a line on a graph, with price on the vertical axis and quantity supplied on the horizontal axis. Each point on the supply curve represents a different price-quantity combination. The shape of the supply curve is determined by the factors that affect supply, such as the cost of inputs, technology, and the number of producers.

Changes in the factors that affect supply can cause the supply curve to shift leftward or rightward. For example, if the cost of inputs increases, the supply curve shifts leftward, indicating a decrease in supply at all price-quantity combinations. If the number of producers increases, the supply curve shifts rightward, indicating an increase in supply at all price-quantity combinations.

The supply curve is an important tool for businesses and policymakers in making decisions related to production, pricing, and regulation. The interaction of supply and demand in a market determines the equilibrium price and quantity of a good or service, which is the point at which the quantity demanded equals the quantity supplied.

The determinants of supply are the factors that affect the quantity of a good or service that producers are willing and able to offer for sale at different prices, over a given time period. Changes in these determinants can cause the supply curve to shift leftward or rightward. The main determinants of supply include:

1. Price of inputs: The cost of the resources used to produce a good or service, such as labor, raw materials, and energy, affects the supply of the good or service. If the cost of inputs increases, the supply curve shifts leftward, indicating a decrease in supply. If the cost of inputs decreases, the supply curve shifts rightward, indicating an increase in supply.
2. Technology: Improvements in technology can lower the cost of production, which increases the supply of a good or service. For example, advances in farming technology can increase crop yields, which increases the supply of agricultural products.
3. Number of producers: The number of producers in a market affects the supply of a good or service. An increase in the number of producers results in an increase in supply, while a decrease in the number of producers results in a decrease in supply.
4. Expectations of future prices: If producers expect the price of a good or service to increase in the future, they may decrease the current supply in order to sell at a higher price in the future.
5. Government policies: Government policies, such as taxes, subsidies, and regulations, can affect the supply of a good or service. For example, a

subsidy for renewable energy production may increase the supply of renewable energy.

6. Production costs: Changes in production costs, such as wages, rent, and interest rates, can affect the supply of a good or service. If production costs increase, the supply curve shifts leftward, indicating a decrease in supply. If production costs decrease, the supply curve shifts rightward, indicating an increase in supply.

7. Climate and weather: In certain markets, such as agriculture, climate and weather can affect the supply of a good or service. Natural disasters or unfavorable weather conditions can decrease supply, while favorable weather conditions can increase supply.

Understanding the determinants of supply is important for businesses and policymakers in making decisions related to production, pricing, and regulation. The interaction of supply and demand in a market determines the equilibrium price and quantity of a good or service.

In economics, a supply function is a mathematical representation of the relationship between the quantity of a good or service that producers are willing and able to supply and the factors that determine the supply, such as price, cost of production, and technology.

The supply function is typically written as:

$Qs = f(P, C, T)$

where Qs represents the quantity of the good or service that producers are willing and able to supply, P represents the price of the good or service, C represents the cost of production, and T represents technology.

The supply function shows the relationship between the quantity supplied and the independent variables, such as price, cost of production, and technology. It is a functional relationship, meaning that a change in any of the independent variables will cause a change in the quantity supplied.

For example, if the cost of production increases, the supply function shifts leftward, indicating a decrease in the quantity supplied at all price levels. Conversely, if technology improves, the supply function shifts rightward, indicating an increase in the quantity supplied at all price levels.

The supply function can be used to determine the supply curve, which is a graphical representation of the relationship between the price of the good or service and the quantity supplied. The supply curve is typically upward-sloping, indicating that as the price of the good or service increases, the quantity supplied also increases.

Understanding the supply function is important for businesses and policymakers in making decisions related to production, pricing, and regulation. By analyzing the determinants of supply and estimating the supply function, businesses and policymakers can make informed decisions about the quantity of the good or service that should be produced and the price at which it should be sold.

Elasticity of supply is a measure of the responsiveness of the quantity supplied of a good or service to changes in its price or other determinants of supply, such as input prices or technology. It is calculated as the percentage change in quantity supplied divided by the percentage change in the price of the good or service or the determinant of supply.

The formula for elasticity of supply is:

Elasticity of supply = (% change in quantity supplied) / (% change in price)

If the elasticity of supply is greater than 1, then the supply is considered elastic, meaning that the quantity supplied is very responsive to changes in price. In other words, a small change in price will result in a large change in the quantity supplied. On the other hand, if the elasticity of supply is less than 1, then the supply is considered inelastic, meaning that the quantity supplied is not very responsive to changes in price. A change in price will result in a proportionally smaller change in the quantity supplied.

If the elasticity of supply is equal to 1, then the supply is considered unit elastic, meaning that the percentage change in the quantity supplied is exactly equal to the percentage change in price.

Factors that affect the elasticity of supply include the availability of inputs, the time horizon for production, and the ability of producers to switch between different goods or services. If inputs are readily available and it is easy to switch between different goods or services, then the supply is likely to be more elastic. However, if inputs are scarce or it takes a long time to adjust production, then the supply is likely to be more inelastic.

Understanding the elasticity of supply is important for businesses and policymakers in making decisions related to production, pricing, and regulation. By analyzing the elasticity of supply, businesses and policymakers can anticipate the responsiveness of the quantity supplied to changes in price and make informed decisions about the quantity of the good or service that should be produced and the price at which it should be sold.

There are three main types of elasticity of supply: elastic, inelastic, and unit elastic.

1. Elastic supply: When the percentage change in quantity supplied is greater than the percentage change in price, supply is said to be elastic. In other words, a small change in price leads to a relatively larger change in quantity supplied. This occurs when producers can easily and quickly adjust their production levels in response to changes in price or other determinants of supply.
2. Inelastic supply: When the percentage change in quantity supplied is less than the percentage change in price, supply is said to be inelastic. In other words, a change in price leads to a relatively smaller change in quantity supplied. This occurs when producers cannot easily and quickly adjust their production levels in response to changes in price or other determinants of supply.
3. Unit elastic supply: When the percentage change in quantity supplied is equal to the percentage change in price, supply is said to be unit elastic. In other words, the change in price leads to an exactly proportional change in quantity supplied. This occurs when producers can adjust their production levels in response to changes in price or other determinants of supply, but the response is not disproportionately large or small.

The elasticity of supply can also be categorized as perfectly elastic or perfectly inelastic, which are extreme cases of elasticity.

4. Perfectly elastic supply: When the quantity supplied changes infinitely in response to any change in price, supply is said to be perfectly elastic. In this case, the supply curve is horizontal and the elasticity of supply is infinite.
5. Perfectly inelastic supply: When the quantity supplied does not change at all in response to changes in price, supply is said to be perfectly inelastic. In this case, the supply curve is vertical and the elasticity of supply is zero.

Understanding the different types of elasticity of supply is important for businesses and policymakers in making decisions related to production, pricing, and regulation. By analyzing the elasticity of supply, businesses and policymakers can anticipate the responsiveness of the quantity supplied to changes in price and make informed decisions about the quantity of the good or service that should be produced and the price at which it should be sold.

1. Example of perfectly elastic supply: Consider a company that produces digital music files. If the price of the music file in the market is $1, the company is willing to supply any quantity of music files as long as the price remains at $1. If the price of the music file decreases by just $0.01, the company is willing to supply an infinite amount of music files. In this case, the price elasticity of supply is perfectly elastic.

2. Example of perfectly inelastic supply: Consider a professional athlete who provides a service of playing in a sports tournament. The athlete can only play a limited number of games in a year and cannot increase the number of games played even if the price increases. In this case, the price elasticity of supply is perfectly inelastic.

3. Example of unit elastic supply: Consider a restaurant that can adjust its daily supply of pizza in response to changes in price. If the price of pizza increases by 10%, the restaurant is willing to increase its daily supply of pizza by 10%. If the price of pizza decreases by 10%, the restaurant is willing to decrease its daily supply of pizza by 10%. In this case, the price elasticity of supply is unit elastic.

4. Example of elastic supply: Consider a company that produces solar panels. If the price of solar panels increases by 10%, the company is able to increase its production of solar panels by 20%. If the price of solar panels decreases by 10%, the company is able to decrease its production of solar panels by 20%. In this case, the price elasticity of supply is elastic.

5. Example of inelastic supply: Consider a company that produces luxury watches. If the price of luxury watches increases by 10%, the company is only able to increase its production of watches by 5%. If the price of luxury watches decreases by 10%, the company is only able to decrease its production of watches by 5%. In this case, the price elasticity of supply is inelastic.

The concepts of demand and supply are essential for understanding the functioning of modern economies. Here are some of the uses of demand and supply in the current world:

1. Setting prices: The forces of demand and supply determine the price of goods and services in a market-based economy. Understanding the demand and supply curves can help businesses and policymakers set prices for goods and services that are in line with market conditions.
2. Allocating resources: The interactions between demand and supply determine the allocation of resources in an economy. Businesses use the signals from the market to allocate resources towards the production of goods and services that are in high demand. Governments can also use market signals to allocate resources towards public goods and services.
3. Policy-making: Policymakers can use the concepts of demand and supply to design policies that can stabilize prices, encourage investment and promote economic growth. For example, the government can use fiscal policies such as taxes and subsidies to influence demand and supply of goods and services.
4. Forecasting: The demand and supply curves can be used to make forecasts about future market conditions. Businesses and policymakers can use these forecasts to make informed decisions about production, pricing and resource allocation.
5. Understanding market dynamics: Understanding the demand and supply curves can help businesses and policymakers understand the dynamics of the market. For example, changes in consumer preferences, technology, and government policies can shift the demand and supply curves, which can impact market outcomes.

Overall, the concepts of demand and supply are crucial for businesses, policymakers, and consumers to make informed decisions and understand how markets work.

1. What is the definition of demand? a) The quantity of a good or service that producers are willing to supply at a given price b) The quantity of a good or service that consumers are willing and able to buy at a given price c) The relationship between price and quantity supplied d) The relationship between price and quantity demanded
2. Which of the following is a determinant of demand? a) Production costs b) Government regulation c) Consumer income d) Technological advancements
3. What happens to the demand curve when there is an increase in consumer income? a) It shifts to the right b) It shifts to the left c) It

becomes steeper d) It becomes flatter

4. What is the definition of supply? a) The quantity of a good or service that producers are willing to supply at a given price b) The quantity of a good or service that consumers are willing and able to buy at a given price c) The relationship between price and quantity supplied d) The relationship between price and quantity demanded

5. Which of the following is a determinant of supply? a) Consumer tastes and preferences b) Changes in the weather c) Government regulation d) Consumer income

6. What happens to the supply curve when there is an increase in the cost of production? a) It shifts to the right b) It shifts to the left c) It becomes steeper d) It becomes flatter

7. What is the law of demand? a) As price increases, quantity demanded decreases b) As price increases, quantity demanded increases c) As quantity demanded increases, price increases d) As quantity demanded decreases, price decreases

8. What is the law of supply? a) As price increases, quantity supplied decreases b) As price increases, quantity supplied increases c) As quantity supplied increases, price decreases d) As quantity supplied decreases, price increases

9. Which of the following is a characteristic of a perfectly competitive market? a) Many buyers and many sellers b) Few buyers and few sellers c) One buyer and many sellers d) One seller and many buyers

10. What is the difference between a change in demand and a change in quantity demanded? a) A change in demand is a shift of the entire demand curve, while a change in quantity demanded is a movement along the demand curve. b) A change in demand is a movement along the demand curve, while a change in quantity demanded is a shift of the entire demand curve. c) A change in demand and a change in quantity demanded are the same thing. d) None of the above.

11. Which of the following is a characteristic of an elastic demand curve? a) The price elasticity of demand is greater than 1 b) The price elasticity of demand is equal to 1 c) The price elasticity of demand is less than 1 d) The price elasticity of demand is undefined

12. Which of the following is a characteristic of an inelastic demand curve? a) The price elasticity of demand is greater than 1 b) The price elasticity of demand is equal to 1 c) The price elasticity of demand is less than 1 d) The price elasticity of demand is undefined

13. Which of the following is a characteristic of a perfectly elastic supply curve? a) The price elasticity of supply is greater than 1 b) The price elasticity of supply is equal to 1 c) The price elasticity of supply is less than 1 d) The price elasticity of supply is undefined

Production is a key concept in economics that refers to the creation of goods and services that satisfy human wants and needs. It involves the transformation of inputs, such as labor, capital, and natural resources, into outputs, such as goods and services, that have value to consumers.

In economics, production is studied at different levels, including the individual level (the production decisions of a single firm or household), the industry level (the production decisions of all firms in a particular industry), and the aggregate level (the production decisions of the entire economy).

Production is influenced by a variety of factors, including the availability and cost of inputs, technological progress, government policies, and market demand. Economists use various models and frameworks, such as production functions and cost curves, to study production and analyze the behavior of firms in different market structures.

Overall, production plays a critical role in economic growth and development, as it creates the goods and services that are essential for human well-being and contributes to the overall prosperity of society.

The factors of production are the resources that are used in the production of goods and services. The four main factors of production are:

1. Land: This includes natural resources, such as forests, water, minerals, and fertile land, that are used to produce goods and services.
2. Labor: This includes the physical and mental effort that is expended by workers in the production process. Labor can be skilled or unskilled and can include both manual and intellectual work.
3. Capital: This includes the tools, machinery, equipment, and infrastructure that are used to produce goods and services. Capital can be physical, such as buildings and machinery, or financial, such as money that is used to purchase inputs.
4. Entrepreneurship: This includes the creativity, innovation, and risk-taking that is involved in starting and running a business. Entrepreneurs are responsible for bringing together the other factors of production and organizing them to produce goods and services.

These four factors of production are essential for economic growth and development. The availability and quality of these factors can impact the productivity and efficiency of firms, which in turn can affect economic output and overall living standards. Governments and policymakers often use various policies and incentives to encourage the development and efficient use of these factors of production.

In economics, a production function is a mathematical expression that describes the relationship between the inputs used in the production process and the output that is produced. It shows how the level of output depends on the quantity and quality of inputs used in the production process.

The general form of a production function is:

$Q = f(L, K, H, N)$

where Q is the quantity of output produced, L is the quantity of labor used, K is the quantity of physical capital used, H is the quantity of human capital used, and N is the quantity of natural resources used.

The production function shows the maximum output that can be produced with a given set of inputs. It assumes that technology is fixed and that there are no changes in the prices of inputs. However, in reality, technology and input prices can change, and firms must adjust their production processes to stay competitive.

The production function can be used to analyze the efficiency of a firm's production process and to determine the optimal combination of inputs that can maximize output. It can also be used to analyze the impact of changes in input prices or changes in technology on the firm's production process.

Overall, the production function is an important tool for economists to understand how the inputs used in the production process interact to create the output that is consumed by society.

The law of variable proportion is an economic principle that states that as the proportion of one input in a production process is increased while holding all other inputs constant, the marginal product of that input will eventually decline, ceteris paribus. This law is also known as the law of diminishing returns.

For example, suppose a firm is producing pizzas and has a fixed amount of capital (e.g., ovens, utensils, etc.) and variable inputs of labor (e.g., workers) and flour. As the firm hires more workers and adds more flour to produce more pizzas, there comes a point where the marginal product of labor (the additional output produced by adding one more worker) starts to decrease. This is because there is only so much space in the kitchen and each additional worker might start to get in each other's way, leading to a decrease in efficiency.

Similarly, the marginal product of flour will also start to decrease as the firm adds more flour, because there are only so many ovens and utensils to work with. Eventually, the additional output produced by adding more inputs will start to decrease and may even become negative, meaning that the firm is now producing less output with each additional unit of input.

The law of variable proportion has important implications for firms as they seek to maximize profits. It suggests that firms should continue to add inputs until the marginal product of each input is equal to its price. Beyond that point, the cost of adding more inputs may outweigh the benefits, leading to lower profits.

In economics, "returns to scale" refers to the relationship between changes in input and output in the production process. Specifically, it refers to how changes in the scale or size of a firm's operations affect its level of output.

There are three types of returns to scale:

1. Increasing returns to scale: This occurs when a proportional increase in all inputs leads to a more than proportional increase in output. For example, if a firm doubles its inputs of labor, capital, and materials, and its output more than doubles, this is an example of increasing returns to scale.
2. Constant returns to scale: This occurs when a proportional increase in all inputs leads to a proportional increase in output. For example, if a firm doubles its inputs and its output also doubles, this is an example of constant returns to scale.
3. Decreasing returns to scale: This occurs when a proportional increase in all inputs leads to a less than proportional increase in output. For example, if a firm doubles its inputs and its output increases by less than double, this is an example of decreasing returns to scale.

The concept of returns to scale is important in understanding how firms can optimize their production processes. For example, if a firm experiences increasing returns to scale, it may benefit from expanding its operations and increasing the scale of its production. However, if a firm experiences decreasing returns to scale, it may benefit from reducing its scale or finding ways to become more efficient in its use of inputs.

In economics, an indifference curve is a graph that represents all combinations of two goods that a consumer views as equally desirable or satisfying, based on their preferences. An indifference curve shows the different combinations of two goods that provide the same level of utility or satisfaction to the consumer.

Indifference curves are typically downward sloping, convex to the origin, and do not intersect. The downward slope of the indifference curve reflects the idea that as a consumer obtains more of one good, they are willing to give up some of that good to obtain more of the other good in order to maintain the same level of satisfaction. The convex shape of the indifference curve reflects the idea of diminishing marginal utility: as a consumer obtains more and more of a good, each additional unit provides less and less additional satisfaction, so they require more and more of the other good to compensate for the diminishing marginal utility of the first good.

Indifference curves are used to analyze consumer behavior and to derive demand curves for different goods. The slope of an indifference curve represents the marginal rate of substitution, or the amount of one good that a consumer is willing to give up for an additional unit of the other good. The slope of the indifference curve at any point is equal to the ratio of the marginal utilities of the two goods at that point.

Indifference curves can also be used to derive a consumer's optimal consumption bundle, which is the combination of two goods that maximizes the consumer's utility subject to their budget constraint. The optimal consumption bundle occurs where the indifference curve is tangent to the budget constraint.

Indifference curves have several properties that help economists analyze consumer behavior and derive demand curves. These properties include:

1. Downward sloping: Indifference curves are downward sloping, which means that as a consumer consumes more of one good, they are willing to give up some of that good to obtain more of the other good in order to maintain the same level of satisfaction.
2. Convex to the origin: Indifference curves are convex to the origin, which means that the marginal rate of substitution, or the amount of one good that a consumer is willing to give up for an additional unit of the other

good, is decreasing as the consumer moves down the curve.

3. Non-intersecting: Indifference curves do not intersect each other. This reflects the idea that each curve represents a different level of satisfaction, and a consumer cannot be indifferent between two bundles that provide different levels of satisfaction.

4. Higher curves represent higher levels of satisfaction: Indifference curves that are further away from the origin represent higher levels of satisfaction. This reflects the idea that as a consumer obtains more of both goods, their total level of satisfaction increases.

5. Indifference curves cannot be thicker: Indifference curves cannot be thicker, which means that the consumer must always be indifferent between any two points on the same curve. This reflects the idea that the consumer has consistent preferences and does not change their mind about the relative desirability of the two goods as they move along the curve.

Isoquants are graphical representations of the combinations of two inputs that yield the same level of output in the production process. They are commonly used to analyze the production process in firms. Here are some of the properties of isoquants:

1. Downward sloping: Like indifference curves, isoquants are downward sloping. This means that as the firm increases the quantity of one input, it can decrease the quantity of the other input while maintaining the same level of output.

2. Convex to the origin: Isoquants are also convex to the origin, which means that the marginal rate of technical substitution, or the amount by which the firm can reduce the quantity of one input for a one-unit increase in the other input while maintaining the same level of output, is diminishing.

3. Do not intersect: Isoquants do not intersect each other. This reflects the idea that each isoquant represents a different level of output, and it is not possible for the firm to produce the same level of output using two different combinations of inputs.

4. Higher isoquants represent higher levels of output: Isoquants that are further away from the origin represent higher levels of output. This reflects the idea that as the firm increases the quantity of both inputs, the level of output produced also increases.

5. Isoquants are smooth and continuous: Isoquants are smooth and continuous, which means that small changes in input quantities result in small changes in output. This reflects the idea that production processes are continuous and do not have sudden jumps in output due to small changes in input quantities.
6. Isoquants cannot intersect axes: Isoquants cannot intersect the axes because the production process requires at least some positive amount of both inputs to produce any output. This means that isoquants cannot start from the origin.

These properties of isoquants help economists and managers understand the production process and make decisions regarding input combinations and output levels.

In economics, costs refer to the expenses incurred in the production process. There are several types of costs that firms must consider:

1. Fixed costs: Fixed costs are costs that do not vary with the level of output. Examples of fixed costs include rent, property taxes, and insurance premiums. These costs are incurred regardless of whether the firm produces anything.
2. Variable costs: Variable costs are costs that vary with the level of output. Examples of variable costs include raw materials, labor, and energy. These costs increase as the firm produces more output.
3. Total costs: Total costs are the sum of fixed costs and variable costs. They increase as the firm produces more output.
4. Average costs: Average costs are the total costs per unit of output. They are calculated by dividing the total cost by the quantity produced.
5. Marginal costs: Marginal costs are the additional costs incurred by producing one more unit of output. They are calculated by taking the change in total cost divided by the change in quantity produced.
6. Explicit costs: Explicit costs are costs that involve a monetary payment. They include expenses such as wages, rent, and utilities.
7. Implicit costs: Implicit costs are costs that do not involve a monetary payment. They include opportunity costs, such as the forgone income from the best alternative use of a resource.
8. Sunk costs: Sunk costs are costs that have already been incurred and cannot be recovered. They should not be considered in making current decisions.

These different types of costs are important for firms to consider when making decisions about production, pricing, and resource allocatio

In economics, a market is a mechanism that facilitates the exchange of goods, services, or resources between buyers and sellers. A market can take many different forms, from a physical location like a bazaar or a mall to a virtual space like an online marketplace or an auction website.

In a market, buyers and sellers interact with each other through the process of exchange, where sellers offer goods or services for a certain price, and buyers either accept the offer or negotiate a different price. The interaction of buyers and sellers determines the market price of the good or service, which reflects the equilibrium point where the quantity of the good or service demanded by buyers is equal to the quantity supplied by sellers.

Markets can be local, regional, national, or international, and can involve a wide range of products and services. The efficiency and competitiveness of a market depends on factors such as the number of buyers and sellers, the level of information available to participants, and the degree of competition among sellers.

A monopoly is a market structure in which a single firm dominates the market, giving it complete control over the price and supply of the product. The following are the features of a monopoly:

1. Single seller: In a monopoly, there is only one firm that produces and sells the product. This means that the firm has complete control over the market and can charge whatever price it wants.
2. No close substitutes: A monopoly has no close substitutes for its product. This means that consumers have no choice but to buy the product from the monopolist, giving the firm even more control over the market.
3. Barriers to entry: A monopoly is characterized by high barriers to entry, which prevent new firms from entering the market and competing with the monopolist. Barriers to entry can include legal barriers, economies of scale, or control over essential resources.
4. Price maker: A monopolist is a price maker, which means that it has the power to set the price of its product. The monopolist will typically charge a price that maximizes its profits, which may not be the same as the price that maximizes consumer welfare.
5. Supernormal profits: A monopoly can earn supernormal profits, which are profits that exceed the normal level of profits in a competitive market. The ability to earn supernormal profits is due to the firm's

control over the market and its ability to charge a higher price than it would in a competitive market.

6. Lack of competition: A monopoly lacks competition, which can lead to a lack of innovation, poor quality products, and higher prices for consumers.

Overall, monopolies are generally considered to be inefficient and harmful to consumer welfare. This is because they restrict output and charge higher prices than would be the case in a competitive market. However, some monopolies may be beneficial if they are able to achieve economies of scale and provide high-quality products at a lower cost than would be possible in a competitive market.

Perfect competition is a market structure in which a large number of small firms compete with each other in a homogenous product market. The following are the features of perfect competition:

1. Large number of buyers and sellers: In a perfect competition market, there are a large number of buyers and sellers, none of whom can influence the price of the product.
2. Homogeneous product: The product sold by all the firms is identical in terms of quality, features, and price.
3. Free entry and exit: In a perfect competition market, firms can freely enter and exit the market without any barriers.
4. Perfect information: All the buyers and sellers have perfect information about the market and the price of the product.
5. Price taker: Each firm is a price taker, which means that it has to accept the market price of the product and cannot influence it.
6. Zero economic profit in the long run: In the long run, a firm operating in a perfect competition market earns zero economic profit. This is because if a firm earns positive economic profit, it attracts new firms into the market, which increases competition and reduces profit.
7. Mobility of resources: Resources are freely mobile in a perfect competition market, which means that they can easily move from one industry to another.
8. No market power: In a perfect competition market, no single buyer or seller has any market power. Each firm is too small to influence the market price.

Overall, perfect competition is considered to be an ideal market structure because it leads to efficient allocation of resources and maximizes consumer welfare. However, in the real world, it is rare to find perfect competition markets as there are often barriers to entry, and products are rarely homogenous.

Monopolistic competition is a market structure in which many firms compete with each other by selling differentiated products that are similar but not identical. The following are the features of monopolistic competition:

1. Large number of buyers and sellers: In a monopolistic competition market, there are a large number of buyers and sellers, but not as many as in a perfect competition market.
2. Differentiated products: The products sold by each firm are differentiated from each other in terms of quality, features, and price.
3. Free entry and exit: Firms can freely enter and exit the market without any barriers.
4. Advertising: Firms engage in advertising to make their products more attractive to consumers.
5. Some market power: Each firm has some market power due to the differentiation of their products, which allows them to set a price higher than the marginal cost of production.
6. Downward sloping demand curve: The demand curve faced by each firm is downward sloping, which means that as the price of the product increases, the quantity demanded decreases.
7. Short-run economic profit: Firms can earn economic profit in the short run due to their market power, but this attracts new firms into the market, which increases competition and reduces profit.
8. Product innovation: Firms engage in product innovation to differentiate their products from their competitors.

Overall, monopolistic competition is a market structure that combines features of both perfect competition and monopoly. It leads to some inefficiencies, such as higher prices and reduced output, but it also promotes innovation and product differentiation.

Oligopoly is a market structure in which a small number of large firms dominate the market. The following are the features of an oligopoly:

1. Few large firms: In an oligopoly market, there are only a few large firms that dominate the market.
2. Interdependence: The behavior of one firm affects the behavior of other firms in the market, which makes them interdependent.
3. Entry barriers: High barriers to entry prevent new firms from entering the market, which helps the existing firms maintain their market power.
4. Product differentiation: Firms engage in product differentiation to make their products appear different from their competitors.
5. Non-price competition: Firms engage in non-price competition, such as advertising, product innovation, and branding, to attract customers.
6. Price rigidity: In an oligopoly market, prices are usually rigid and do not change frequently.
7. Collusion: Firms may collude with each other to increase their profits by fixing prices, dividing the market, or limiting production.
8. Game theory: Oligopolies use game theory to analyze the behavior of their rivals and to make strategic decisions.

Overall, oligopoly is a market structure that is characterized by a small number of large firms that dominate the market. It leads to higher prices, reduced output, and less innovation compared to a competitive market, but it also promotes efficiency through economies of scale and barriers to entry.

1. Which of the following is NOT a type of market?

   A. Monopoly
   B. Oligopoly
   C. Capitalism
   D. Perfect competition
   Answer: C. Capitalism

2. What is a monopoly market?

   A. A market where there are many sellers but only one buyer
   B. A market where there is only one seller and many buyers
   C. A market where there is perfect competition
   D. A market where there are a few large sellers and many buyers
   Answer: B. A market where there is only one seller and many buyers

3. What is a characteristic of an oligopoly market?

A. There is only one seller in the market
B. There are many sellers in the market
C. There is perfect competition in the market
D. There are a few large sellers in the market
Answer: D. There are a few large sellers in the market

4. What is the primary goal of production?

A. To maximize profits
B. To satisfy consumer demand
C. To minimize costs
D. To increase market share
Answer: B. To satisfy consumer demand

5. What is the difference between capital goods and consumer goods?

A. Capital goods are used to produce consumer goods, while consumer goods are used by individuals or households
B. Capital goods are used by individuals or households, while consumer goods are used to produce other goods
C. Capital goods and consumer goods are the same thing
D. Capital goods are produced by businesses, while consumer goods are produced by governments
Answer: A. Capital goods are used to produce consumer goods, while consumer goods are used by individuals or households.

6. Which of the following is a characteristic of a perfectly competitive market?

A. Many buyers and many sellers
B. One buyer and many sellers
C. One seller and many buyers
D. Few buyers and few sellers
Answer: A. Many buyers and many sellers

7. In a monopolistic competition market, what differentiates products?

A. Price
B. Quality
C. Advertising
D. All of the above
Answer: D. All of the above

8. What is the difference between a natural monopoly and a legal monopoly?

A. A natural monopoly is created by the government, while a legal monopoly occurs naturally
B. A natural monopoly is regulated by the government, while a legal monopoly is not C. A natural monopoly occurs when one firm can produce goods or services at a lower cost than any other firm, while a legal monopoly occurs when the government grants exclusive rights to produce a good or service
D. A natural monopoly occurs when there is perfect competition, while a legal monopoly occurs when there is a lack of competition
Answer: C. A natural monopoly occurs when one firm can produce goods or services at a lower cost than any other firm, while a legal monopoly occurs when the government grants exclusive rights to produce a good or service

9. What is the difference between labor productivity and capital productivity?

A. Labor productivity is the output per worker, while capital productivity is the output per unit of capital
B. Labor productivity is the output per unit of capital, while capital productivity is the output per worker
C. Labor productivity and capital productivity are the same thing
D. Labor productivity is the output per hour worked, while capital productivity is the output per day worked
Answer: A. Labor productivity is the output per worker, while capital productivity is the output per unit of capital

10. What is the difference between a fixed cost and a variable cost?

A. Fixed costs vary with the level of production, while variable costs remain constant B. Fixed costs remain constant, while variable costs vary with the level of production C. Fixed costs and variable costs are the same thing

D. Fixed costs are direct costs, while variable costs are indirect costs

Answer: B. Fixed costs remain constant, while variable costs vary with the level of production.

CHAPTER THREE

Macroeconomics

Macroeconomics This chapter will cover the principles of macroeconomics, including national income, inflation, monetary policy, fiscal policy, and international trade.

Macroeconomics is the branch of economics that studies the behavior of the entire economy, rather than individual markets or firms. It deals with the aggregate performance of the economy as a whole, including topics such as economic growth, inflation, unemployment, and fiscal and monetary policy.

Macroeconomics looks at the relationships between various economic variables such as gross domestic product (GDP), consumption, investment, and government spending. It also examines how changes in these variables affect economic outcomes such as inflation, unemployment, and economic growth.

Macroeconomics is concerned with understanding the overall behavior of the economy, and how policies such as monetary and fiscal policies can be used to manage the economy and achieve desirable outcomes. It is an important field of study for governments, policymakers, and businesses, as it provides insights into how the economy functions and how it can be managed for the benefit of society as a whole.

Macroeconomics plays a significant role in everyday life, as it affects many aspects of our lives, including employment, income, prices, and the overall standard of living. Here are some examples of how macroeconomics affects everyday life:

1. Employment: Macroeconomic factors such as economic growth, inflation, and interest rates can affect employment levels. During periods of economic growth, businesses may hire more workers, leading to lower unemployment rates. Conversely, during economic downturns,

businesses may lay off workers, resulting in higher unemployment rates.

2. Income: Macroeconomic factors such as GDP and inflation can impact household income. A strong economy with high GDP growth can lead to higher incomes for workers, while inflation can erode the purchasing power of wages.

3. Prices: Macroeconomic factors such as inflation and supply and demand can affect the prices of goods and services. Higher inflation can lead to higher prices for goods and services, while changes in supply and demand can also impact prices.

4. Investments: Macroeconomic factors such as interest rates, economic growth, and government policies can impact investment decisions. For example, when interest rates are low, it may be more attractive for investors to invest in stocks or real estate, while higher interest rates may make it more attractive to save money in bonds or other fixed-income securities.

5. Government Policies: Macroeconomic policies such as fiscal and monetary policies can impact the overall health of the economy and influence economic outcomes such as inflation and employment. For example, government stimulus packages aimed at boosting economic growth can lead to increased consumer spending and higher employment rates.

Overall, macroeconomics plays an important role in shaping our daily lives, as it affects many of the economic factors that impact our standard of living.

The circular flow of income is a concept in macroeconomics that shows how money flows between households, firms, and government in a market economy. The circular flow model demonstrates the interdependence between different sectors of the economy and how they are linked through various transactions.

The circular flow model consists of two sectors: the household sector and the business sector. The household sector consists of individuals and families who consume goods and services, while the business sector consists of firms that produce and sell goods and services. The government sector is also included in the model, as it collects taxes and provides public goods and services.

In the circular flow model, households supply factors of production such as labor, land, and capital to firms in exchange for wages, rent, and profits.

These factors are used by firms to produce goods and services, which are then sold to households in exchange for payment.

The money flows between households and firms in the form of consumer spending and revenue generated from the sale of goods and services. This money is then used by firms to pay for the factors of production supplied by households, such as wages and rent.

The government sector also plays a role in the circular flow of income by collecting taxes from households and firms and using the revenue to provide public goods and services, such as roads, schools, and healthcare. Government spending on these goods and services also creates a flow of income, as it provides employment and income for those who produce and provide these goods and services.

In summary, the circular flow of income shows the flow of money and goods and services between households, firms, and government in a market economy. The model demonstrates how these different sectors of the economy are interdependent and how they contribute to economic growth and development.

National income is the total value of all goods and services produced within a country over a specific period of time, usually one year. It is an important measure of a country's economic performance and is often used to compare the economic performance of different countries.

Here are some key terms related to national income:

1. Gross Domestic Product (GDP): GDP is the total value of all goods and services produced within a country's borders, regardless of the nationality of the producers. It is the most commonly used measure of national income.
2. Gross National Product (GNP): GNP is the total value of all goods and services produced by a country's residents, regardless of where they are produced. It includes income earned by citizens and businesses both domestically and abroad.
3. Net National Product (NNP): NNP is the total value of all goods and services produced by a country's residents, minus the depreciation of capital goods used in the production process.
4. National Income (NI): NI is the total income earned by a country's residents, including wages, salaries, rent, and profits.
5. Personal Income (PI): PI is the income received by households and individuals, including wages, salaries, and transfer payments such as

Social Security and welfare benefits.

6. Disposable Income (DI): DI is the income that households and individuals have available for consumption and saving after taxes have been paid.

There are three main methods used to measure Gross Domestic Product (GDP), which is the total value of all goods and services produced within a country's borders over a specific period of time, usually one year. These methods are:

1. Output method: This method involves adding up the total value of all final goods and services produced in a country during a specific period of time. This includes all goods and services produced by all sectors of the economy, including agriculture, manufacturing, and services.
2. Income method: This method involves adding up all the income earned by households and businesses in the country during a specific period of time. This includes wages, salaries, profits, rent, and interest income. The total income earned by households and businesses is equivalent to the total value of all goods and services produced in the country.
3. Expenditure method: This method involves adding up all the spending on final goods and services in the country during a specific period of time. This includes consumer spending, investment spending by businesses, government spending, and spending by foreigners on exports. The total spending on goods and services is equivalent to the total value of all goods and services produced in the country.

In practice, these three methods are used in combination to measure GDP, as they provide different perspectives on the economy and can help to cross-check the accuracy of the data. For example, the output method can be used to measure the value of goods produced in the manufacturing sector, while the income method can be used to measure the value of services produced in the service sector. By combining these methods, economists can get a comprehensive picture of the economy and how it is performing over time.

The national income estimates in India are typically measured and reported by the Central Statistics Office (CSO) under the Ministry of Statistics and Programme Implementation. The CSO uses various methods and data sources to estimate the country's national income, including data from surveys, administrative records, and other sources.

The CSO produces various measures of national income, including Gross Domestic Product (GDP), Gross Value Added (GVA), and Net National Income (NNI), among others. These estimates are typically reported on an annual basis, as well as broken down by various sectors of the economy, such as agriculture, industry, and services.

The latest available estimates for India's national income can be found on the website of the Ministry of Statistics and Programme Implementation.

The measurement and estimation of national income in India has a long and evolving history. Here's a brief overview:

- Pre-Independence era: Prior to India's independence in 1947, there were no comprehensive estimates of national income. However, some early efforts to estimate the size of the Indian economy were made by British economists, such as Dadabhai Naoroji and William Digby.

- Post-Independence era: After India gained independence, the first official estimates of national income were produced by the Central Statistical Organisation (CSO) in 1950. These estimates were based on limited data sources, such as agricultural output and industrial production.

- 1950s and 1960s: During this period, the CSO refined its estimation methods and began to use more comprehensive data sources, such as surveys of household consumption and expenditure. The CSO also developed new measures of national income, such as Gross Domestic Product (GDP) and Gross National Product (GNP).

- 1970s and 1980s: In the 1970s, the CSO began to produce estimates of sector-wise national income, which broke down GDP by industry and service sectors. In the 1980s, the CSO introduced new measures of national income, such as Net National Product (NNP) and Net Domestic Product (NDP).

- 1990s and beyond: In the 1990s, India began to implement economic reforms that liberalized the economy and stimulated growth. The CSO continued to refine its methods of measuring national income, and in 2015, it introduced a new series of GDP estimates based on updated data sources and methodologies.

Today, the CSO continues to produce regular estimates of national income in India, using a variety of data sources and methods. These estimates are important for policymakers, businesses, and researchers who seek to understand the size and growth of the Indian economy.

Inflation refers to a sustained increase in the general price level of goods and services in an economy over a period of time. Inflation is typically measured using an inflation index, which tracks the price changes of a basket of goods and services that are representative of the economy as a whole.

Inflation can have various causes, including:

- Increase in demand: If the demand for goods and services in an economy increases, but the supply remains the same, the prices will go up, leading to inflation.
- Increase in production costs: If the costs of producing goods and services increase, producers may raise their prices to maintain their profit margins.
- Increase in the money supply: If the central bank of a country prints more money and puts it into circulation, there will be more money chasing the same amount of goods and services, leading to inflation.
- External factors: Changes in the exchange rate, international commodity prices, or other external factors can also affect inflation in a country.

Inflation can have both positive and negative effects on an economy. Some level of inflation is necessary for economic growth, as it encourages investment and consumption by making borrowing cheaper. However, high levels of inflation can be damaging to an economy, as it erodes the purchasing power of the currency and makes it difficult for businesses and households to plan for the future.

Central banks and governments typically use various tools to control inflation, such as adjusting interest rates, implementing fiscal policies, and regulating the money supply.

There are several types of inflation that can occur in an economy. Here are some common types:

1. Demand-pull inflation: This occurs when the demand for goods and services in an economy outstrips the supply, causing prices to rise. This type of inflation can be caused by factors such as strong economic growth, increases in government spending, or expansionary monetary policies.

2. Cost-push inflation: This type of inflation occurs when there is a rise in the cost of production, such as wages or raw materials, which leads to an increase in the prices of goods and services. Cost-push inflation can be caused by factors such as supply shocks, such as a natural disaster that disrupts production, or increases in taxes or regulations that raise costs for businesses.

3. Built-in inflation: This occurs when workers and businesses build inflation expectations into their decisions, causing wages and prices to rise even in the absence of any actual increase in demand or production costs. This type of inflation can be difficult to control, as it becomes a self-fulfilling prophecy.

4. Hyperinflation: This is an extreme form of inflation, where prices rise at a very high rate, often reaching hundreds or even thousands of percent per year. Hyperinflation can be caused by a variety of factors, such as a collapse in the value of the currency, excessive government spending, or a loss of confidence in the economy.

5. Structural inflation: This occurs when there is a long-term mismatch between the supply and demand of goods and services in an economy, leading to sustained inflation. Structural inflation can be caused by factors such as a lack of investment in productive capacity, bottlenecks in the supply chain, or persistent deficits in trade or government finances.

Understanding the types of inflation can help policymakers develop appropriate responses to control inflation and minimize its negative impacts on the economy.

In India, inflation is primarily measured using the Wholesale Price Index (WPI) and the Consumer Price Index (CPI). Here's a brief overview of these methods:

1. Wholesale Price Index (WPI): The WPI measures the average price changes of goods that are traded in bulk at the wholesale level. The index is based on a basket of goods that are representative of the economy, such as food items, fuel, and raw materials. The WPI is calculated by taking the weighted average of the prices of these goods.

2. Consumer Price Index (CPI): The CPI measures the average price changes of goods and services that are consumed by households. The index is based on a basket of goods and services that are representative

of the consumption patterns of different groups of households. The CPI is calculated by taking the weighted average of the prices of these goods and services.

The Indian government uses both the WPI and the CPI to track inflation and make policy decisions. The CPI is more commonly used as a measure of inflation for policy purposes, as it is seen as a better indicator of the impact of inflation on households.

In addition to the WPI and CPI, the Reserve Bank of India (RBI) also uses other methods to measure inflation, such as the GDP deflator, which measures the price changes of all goods and services produced in the economy, and the Core Inflation Index, which excludes volatile components like food and fuel from the CPI basket to give a more stable measure of inflation.

Overall, inflation measurement in India is a complex process that involves multiple methods and data sources. The government and RBI regularly review and update these methods to ensure that inflation is accurately measured and policy decisions are based on reliable data.

The GDP deflator is a measure of the level of prices for all goods and services produced in an economy, and is used to adjust the nominal Gross Domestic Product (GDP) to real GDP. It measures the extent to which the overall price level has changed since the base year, and is calculated as the ratio of nominal GDP to real GDP multiplied by 100.

The GDP deflator is different from other inflation measures, such as the Consumer Price Index (CPI) or Wholesale Price Index (WPI), which only track price changes for specific baskets of goods and services. The GDP deflator, on the other hand, covers all goods and services produced within an economy, and is therefore a broader measure of inflation.

The GDP deflator is used to adjust nominal GDP for inflation, which allows economists and policymakers to compare economic growth and output over time. For example, if nominal GDP increases by 5% in a year, but the GDP deflator shows that prices have risen by 3%, the real GDP growth would be 2%. This adjustment provides a more accurate picture of the changes in the economy's output.

The GDP deflator is also used to compare the level of prices across different countries. As it measures the overall price level of an economy, it can be used to compare the purchasing power of different currencies.

Overall, the GDP deflator is an important measure of inflation and economic growth, as it provides a broad and comprehensive view of price changes in an economy.

The GDP deflator is a measure of the level of prices for all goods and services produced in an economy, and is used to adjust the nominal Gross Domestic Product (GDP) to real GDP. It measures the extent to which the overall price level has changed since the base year, and is calculated as the ratio of nominal GDP to real GDP multiplied by 100.

The GDP deflator is different from other inflation measures, such as the Consumer Price Index (CPI) or Wholesale Price Index (WPI), which only track price changes for specific baskets of goods and services. The GDP deflator, on the other hand, covers all goods and services produced within an economy, and is therefore a broader measure of inflation.

The GDP deflator is used to adjust nominal GDP for inflation, which allows economists and policymakers to compare economic growth and output over time. For example, if nominal GDP increases by 5% in a year, but the GDP deflator shows that prices have risen by 3%, the real GDP growth would be 2%. This adjustment provides a more accurate picture of the changes in the economy's output.

The GDP deflator is also used to compare the level of prices across different countries. As it measures the overall price level of an economy, it can be used to compare the purchasing power of different currencies.

Overall, the GDP deflator is an important measure of inflation and economic growth, as it provides a broad and comprehensive view of price changes in an economy.

Let's assume that the nominal Gross Domestic Product (GDP) of an economy in a given year is Rs. 10,000 crore, and the real GDP is Rs. 8,000 crore. We can use these values to calculate the GDP deflator as follows:

GDP Deflator = (Nominal GDP / Real GDP) x 100

= (10,000 / 8,000) x 100

= 125

This means that the overall price level in the economy has increased by 25% since the base year used to calculate the real GDP.

For example, if the base year real GDP was calculated using the prices of goods and services in the year 2010, and the nominal GDP was calculated using the prices of the same goods and services in the year 2020, the GDP deflator of 125 indicates that prices have increased by 25% over the past 10 years.

This adjustment for inflation using the GDP deflator allows us to compare the real output of an economy over time and across different countries, as it gives us a more accurate picture of changes in the economy's output after adjusting for changes in the price level.

Monetary policy refers to the actions undertaken by a central bank to regulate the supply and cost of money in an economy to achieve macroeconomic objectives such as price stability, economic growth, and full employment. In this essay, we will discuss the various instruments of monetary policy that are used by central banks to achieve these objectives.

1. Open market operations: This is the most common instrument of monetary policy used by central banks. Open market operations involve the purchase or sale of government securities in the open market to influence the level of reserves held by commercial banks. When the central bank buys government securities from banks, it injects liquidity into the banking system, increasing the reserves held by banks and thus stimulating lending and investment. Conversely, when the central bank sells government securities, it drains liquidity from the banking system, reducing the reserves held by banks and thus discouraging lending and investment.

2. Reserve requirement: The central bank sets a reserve requirement, which is the amount of funds that commercial banks are required to hold as reserves against their deposits. By adjusting the reserve requirement, the central bank can influence the amount of funds available for lending by banks. When the reserve requirement is increased, banks are required to hold a larger proportion of their deposits as reserves, reducing the amount of funds available for lending. Conversely, when the reserve requirement is decreased, banks are required to hold a smaller proportion of their deposits as reserves, increasing the amount of funds available for lending.

3. Discount rate: The discount rate is the interest rate at which commercial banks can borrow funds from the central bank. By adjusting the discount rate, the central bank can influence the cost of borrowing for banks and thus the amount of funds available for lending. When the discount rate is decreased, banks can borrow funds at a lower cost, increasing the amount of funds available for lending. Conversely, when the discount rate is increased, banks can borrow funds at a higher cost, reducing the amount of funds available for lending.

4. Interest rate on reserves: The central bank pays interest on the reserves held by commercial banks. By adjusting the interest rate on reserves, the central bank can influence the cost of holding reserves and thus the amount of funds available for lending. When the interest rate on reserves is increased, banks are incentivized to hold more reserves, reducing the amount of funds available for lending. Conversely, when the interest rate on reserves is decreased, banks are incentivized to hold fewer reserves, increasing the amount of funds available for lending.

5. Forward guidance: Central banks also use forward guidance to influence expectations about future monetary policy. This involves communicating to the public the likely direction of monetary policy in the future, which can influence investment and consumption decisions. For example, if the central bank indicates that it is likely to keep interest rates low for an extended period, this can encourage households and businesses to borrow and invest more.

6. Quantitative easing: Quantitative easing involves the purchase of large quantities of long-term government bonds or other securities to inject liquidity into the economy. This can be used as an unconventional tool of monetary policy when interest rates are already at or near zero. By purchasing these securities, the central bank can lower long-term interest rates and encourage investment and consumption.

In conclusion, central banks use a range of instruments to implement monetary policy and achieve macroeconomic objectives. Open market operations, reserve requirements, discount rates, interest rates on reserves, forward guidance, and quantitative easing are some of the tools that central banks use to regulate the supply and cost of money in an economy. The appropriate use of these instruments depends on the specific economic conditions and policy goals of each country.

Fiscal policy refers to the use of government spending and taxation to influence the economy. It is one of the two main tools used by governments to achieve macroeconomic objectives, alongside monetary policy. Fiscal policy can be expansionary or contractionary, depending on whether the government is trying to stimulate or cool down the economy. In this essay, we will discuss the various instruments of fiscal policy that are used by governments to achieve macroeconomic objectives.

1. Government spending: Government spending is a key instrument of fiscal policy. By increasing or decreasing government spending, the government can influence the level of aggregate demand in the economy. When the government spends more, it increases the demand for goods and services, stimulating economic growth. Conversely, when the government spends less, it reduces the demand for goods and services, cooling down the economy. Government spending can be targeted towards specific sectors or groups to achieve specific policy goals, such as infrastructure investment to stimulate economic growth or social welfare programs to reduce inequality.

2. Taxation: Taxation is another key instrument of fiscal policy. By changing tax rates or introducing new taxes, the government can influence the disposable income of households and the profits of businesses, thereby affecting their spending and investment decisions. When taxes are reduced, households and businesses have more disposable income, increasing their spending and investment. Conversely, when taxes are increased, households and businesses have less disposable income, reducing their spending and investment. Taxation can also be used to achieve specific policy goals, such as taxing carbon emissions to reduce environmental pollution or implementing progressive tax systems to reduce inequality.

3. Transfer payments: Transfer payments refer to payments made by the government to individuals or households for reasons other than the purchase of goods or services. Examples of transfer payments include social security benefits, unemployment insurance, and welfare programs. By increasing or decreasing transfer payments, the government can influence the disposable income of households, thereby affecting their spending decisions. When transfer payments are increased, households have more disposable income, increasing their spending. Conversely, when transfer payments are decreased, households have less disposable income, reducing their spending.

4. Public debt: Public debt refers to the amount of money that the government owes to creditors. By borrowing money, the government can finance its spending when tax revenues are insufficient. However, public debt can also have negative consequences, such as increasing interest payments and crowding out private investment. The government can use fiscal policy to manage public debt by implementing policies that reduce the budget deficit, such as cutting spending or

increasing taxes.

5. Automatic stabilizers: Automatic stabilizers refer to changes in government spending and taxation that occur automatically in response to changes in economic conditions. For example, when the economy enters a recession, tax revenues automatically decline as incomes fall and unemployment rises. At the same time, government spending on transfer payments automatically increases as more people become eligible for social welfare programs. These automatic stabilizers help to stabilize the economy without the need for explicit policy interventions.

6. Fiscal rules: Fiscal rules refer to guidelines or targets that governments set for themselves to ensure fiscal sustainability and responsibility. For example, a government may set a target to keep the budget deficit below a certain percentage of GDP or to maintain a certain level of public debt. Fiscal rules help to promote long-term stability and reduce the risk of fiscal crises.

In conclusion, fiscal policy is a key tool used by governments to influence the economy. Government spending, taxation, transfer payments, public debt, automatic stabilizers, and fiscal rules are some of the instruments that governments use to achieve macroeconomic objectives such as economic growth, full employment, and price stability. The appropriate use of these instruments depends on the specific economic conditions and policy goals of each country.

A bank is a financial institution that provides a range of financial services to its customers, including accepting deposits, making loans, and providing other financial services such as credit cards, investment products, and insurance. Banks are important institutions in the economy because they play a critical role in the financial system by channeling funds from savers to borrowers, facilitating transactions, and providing financial services to businesses and households.

There are several types of banks, including commercial banks, investment banks, central banks, and online banks. Commercial banks are the most common type of bank and offer a range of services to customers, including checking and savings accounts, loans, and credit cards. Investment banks, on the other hand, specialize in helping companies raise capital by underwriting securities such as stocks and bonds. Central banks are responsible for regulating the money supply and interest rates in the economy, while online banks operate solely over the internet.

Banks play a crucial role in the economy by providing financing for businesses and individuals. For businesses, banks provide loans to finance operations, purchase equipment, and expand operations. Banks also provide credit to individuals for personal use, such as buying a car or a house. Additionally, banks facilitate transactions between buyers and sellers by processing payments and providing financial services such as wire transfers and online banking.

Banks also play a critical role in the economy by managing the money supply and controlling inflation. Central banks are responsible for regulating the money supply in the economy, which they can do by adjusting interest rates or buying and selling government securities. By regulating the money supply, central banks can help to control inflation and ensure that the economy remains stable.

Overall, banks play a critical role in the economy by providing financial services to businesses and individuals, facilitating transactions, and managing the money supply. The health of the banking sector is closely tied to the health of the overall economy, and policymakers often rely on banks to help manage economic crises and promote growth.

There are several types of banks, each with its own specific functions and services. Here are some of the most common types of banks:

1. Commercial Banks: These banks are the most common type of bank and offer a range of financial services to individuals and businesses, including checking and savings accounts, loans, and credit cards.
2. Investment Banks: These banks specialize in helping companies and governments raise capital by underwriting securities such as stocks and bonds. Investment banks also provide financial advisory services such as mergers and acquisitions and corporate restructuring.
3. Central Banks: These banks are responsible for regulating the money supply and interest rates in an economy. Central banks also supervise and regulate other banks and financial institutions.
4. Retail Banks: These banks cater to individual customers and provide services such as savings and checking accounts, personal loans, and mortgages.
5. Online Banks: These banks operate entirely online, and customers can access their accounts through a website or mobile app. Online banks typically offer higher interest rates on savings accounts and lower fees than traditional banks.

6. Credit Unions: These are member-owned financial cooperatives that offer services similar to those of traditional banks. Credit unions typically offer better interest rates on loans and credit cards and lower fees than traditional banks.
7. Cooperative Banks: These banks are owned and operated by their members, who are typically individuals or businesses in a specific geographic area. Cooperative banks provide a range of financial services to their members, including savings and checking accounts, loans, and credit cards.
8. Private Banks: These banks offer personalized banking and wealth management services to high-net-worth individuals and families.
9. Islamic Banks: These banks operate according to Islamic law, which prohibits the payment or receipt of interest. Instead, Islamic banks provide financing through profit-sharing arrangements, leasing, and other non-interest-based transactions.
10. Development Banks: These banks provide long-term financing for infrastructure and development projects, typically in emerging markets. Development banks are often funded by governments or international organizations.

Top of Form

The Reserve Bank of India (RBI) is the central bank of India and is responsible for regulating the country's monetary policy and currency. The RBI was established in 1935 and is headquartered in Mumbai. The bank is governed by a central board of directors and is headed by a governor.

The primary functions of the RBI include:

1. Regulating the supply of money in the economy through monetary policy, which includes setting interest rates and controlling the money supply.
2. Regulating and supervising the banking system in India, including issuing licenses to banks, setting guidelines for their operations, and conducting inspections and audits.
3. Managing the foreign exchange reserves of the country and regulating foreign exchange transactions.
4. Issuing and managing the country's currency, including designing and printing banknotes and coins.

5. Conducting research and analysis on economic and financial issues and publishing reports and data related to the economy.
6. Advising the government on economic and financial issues and participating in policy formulation.

The RBI is also responsible for maintaining financial stability in the economy, which includes monitoring risks and taking steps to mitigate them. The bank works closely with other regulatory authorities, such as the Securities and Exchange Board of India (SEBI) and the Insurance Regulatory and Development Authority (IRDA), to maintain financial stability.

In addition to its regulatory functions, the RBI also provides a range of banking services to the government and other banks, including managing the government's accounts, providing credit to banks, and facilitating the settlement of interbank transactions.

Overall, the RBI plays a crucial role in India's economy by regulating monetary policy, supervising the banking system, managing the country's currency, and maintaining financial stability. The bank's policies and actions have a significant impact on the Indian economy and are closely watched by investors, businesses, and policymakers.

The Reserve Bank of India (RBI) was established on April 1, 1935, in accordance with the Reserve Bank of India Act, 1934. The bank was established to regulate the currency and credit system in India and to promote the development of the country's financial infrastructure. The RBI was modeled after the Bank of England and was established as a central bank with the authority to issue and manage the country's currency.

The idea of establishing a central bank in India was first proposed by the Hilton Young Commission in 1926. The commission recommended the establishment of a central bank to regulate the country's currency and credit system and to provide a stable and secure financial system. The recommendation was accepted by the Indian government, and the Reserve Bank of India Act was passed in 1934.

The RBI was originally headquartered in Kolkata (then known as Calcutta), but it was moved to Mumbai in 1937. The first governor of the RBI was Sir Osborne Smith, who served from 1935 to 1937.

In the early years of its existence, the RBI focused on stabilizing the currency and credit system in India. The bank was also responsible for managing the government's finances and providing credit to commercial banks. The RBI played a crucial role in the Indian economy during the Second World War when it helped the government finance the war effort.

After India gained independence in 1947, the RBI's role expanded to include promoting economic growth and development. The bank played a key role in developing the country's financial infrastructure, including establishing a network of commercial banks and setting up institutions such as the Industrial Development Bank of India and the National Bank for Agriculture and Rural Development.

Over the years, the RBI's role has continued to evolve. Today, the bank is responsible for regulating monetary policy, supervising the banking system, managing the country's currency, and maintaining financial stability. The RBI's policies and actions have a significant impact on the Indian economy and are closely watched by investors, businesses, and policymakers.

Bottom of Form

Top of Form

The stock market, also known as the equity market, is a marketplace where shares of publicly traded companies are bought and sold. These shares represent ownership in the company and give shareholders a claim on the company's assets and earnings. The stock market provides a means for companies to raise capital by issuing shares to the public, and for investors to buy and sell those shares in order to earn a return on their investment.

The stock market can be divided into two main categories: primary market and secondary market. The primary market is where companies issue new shares to the public through an initial public offering (IPO). The secondary market is where previously issued shares are bought and sold among investors.

The major stock exchanges in India include the Bombay Stock Exchange (BSE) and the National Stock Exchange (NSE). These exchanges provide a platform for companies to list their shares and for investors to buy and sell those shares.

The price of a stock is determined by supply and demand in the market. If there is high demand for a particular stock, the price will go up, and if there is low demand, the price will go down. Factors that can affect demand for a stock include the company's financial performance, industry trends, and macroeconomic factors such as interest rates and inflation.

Investors in the stock market can earn a return on their investment through two main ways: capital gains and dividends. Capital gains are the profits earned by selling a stock at a higher price than the purchase price, while dividends are a share of the company's profits that are distributed to shareholders.

However, investing in the stock market carries risks as well. The value of stocks can be volatile and subject to sudden fluctuations, and investors can lose money if the price of the stock they own goes down. It is important for investors to do their research, diversify their portfolio, and invest for the long term in order to mitigate these risks.

Overall, the stock market plays a crucial role in the Indian economy by providing a means for companies to raise capital and for investors to earn a return on their investment.

The stock market, also known as the equity market, is a marketplace where shares of publicly traded companies are bought and sold. These shares represent ownership in the company and give shareholders a claim on the company's assets and earnings. The stock market provides a means for companies to raise capital by issuing shares to the public, and for investors to buy and sell those shares in order to earn a return on their investment.

The stock market can be divided into two main categories: primary market and secondary market. The primary market is where companies issue new shares to the public through an initial public offering (IPO). The secondary market is where previously issued shares are bought and sold among investors.

The major stock exchanges in India include the Bombay Stock Exchange (BSE) and the National Stock Exchange (NSE). These exchanges provide a platform for companies to list their shares and for investors to buy and sell those shares.

The price of a stock is determined by supply and demand in the market. If there is high demand for a particular stock, the price will go up, and if there is low demand, the price will go down. Factors that can affect demand for a stock include the company's financial performance, industry trends, and macroeconomic factors such as interest rates and inflation.

Investors in the stock market can earn a return on their investment through two main ways: capital gains and dividends. Capital gains are the profits earned by selling a stock at a higher price than the purchase price, while dividends are a share of the company's profits that are distributed to shareholders.

However, investing in the stock market carries risks as well. The value of stocks can be volatile and subject to sudden fluctuations, and investors can lose money if the price of the stock they own goes down. It is important for investors to do their research, diversify their portfolio, and invest for the long term in order to mitigate these risks.

Overall, the stock market plays a crucial role in the Indian economy by providing a means for companies to raise capital and for investors to earn a return on their investment.

Non-financial markets are markets where goods and services are bought and sold. Unlike financial markets, which deal with financial instruments such as stocks and bonds, non-financial markets deal with physical goods and services that are used in the production of other goods and services.

There are several types of non-financial markets, including:

1. Product markets: These are markets where finished goods and services are bought and sold. Examples include the market for cars, clothing, food, and healthcare services.
2. Labor markets: These are markets where labor services are bought and sold. Employers buy the labor services of workers, who in turn sell their labor to earn wages or salaries. Labor markets can be segmented by skill level, industry, and geography.
3. Real estate markets: These are markets where real estate properties such as land, buildings, and homes are bought and sold. Real estate markets can be segmented by location, property type, and price.
4. Commodity markets: These are markets where raw materials such as oil, metals, and agricultural products are bought and sold. Commodity markets can be segmented by product type and geographic region.
5. Auction markets: These are markets where goods and services are sold through an auction process. Auction markets can be physical or online, and may include antiques, art, and collectibles.

Non-financial markets play a crucial role in the economy by facilitating the exchange of goods and services between producers and consumers. The efficiency and competitiveness of non-financial markets can have a significant impact on the overall productivity and growth of the economy.

Unified Payments Interface (UPI) is a digital payment system developed by the National Payments Corporation of India (NPCI). It allows users to transfer money from one bank account to another instantly using a mobile app or through other digital payment channels.

UPI is a real-time payment system that enables transactions 24x7, 365 days a year. It is a highly secure and convenient way to transfer funds, and does not require users to share their bank details or other sensitive information. Instead, users can create a Virtual Payment Address (VPA) that can be shared with others to receive payments.

To use UPI, users need to link their bank account to a UPI-enabled mobile app, which can be downloaded from the app store. Once the app is installed, users can create a UPI ID and set a UPI PIN to initiate transactions. UPI also supports various payment methods, including QR codes, bank account numbers, and mobile numbers.

One of the key benefits of UPI is its interoperability, which means that users can transfer funds between different banks using a single mobile app. UPI has been widely adopted in India, and is accepted by a large number of merchants and service providers, including online retailers, utility companies, and government agencies.

Overall, UPI has revolutionized the way digital payments are made in India, and has played a significant role in promoting financial inclusion and digitalization of the economy.

There are currently two types of UPI available in India:

1. Single Factor Authentication UPI: This type of UPI is designed for transactions up to Rs. 2,000 per transaction. It requires a single factor authentication, such as a mobile PIN, to complete the transaction. Single factor authentication UPI is meant for small transactions and is widely used for peer-to-peer (P2P) transactions.

2. Two Factor Authentication UPI: This type of UPI is designed for transactions above Rs. 2,000 per transaction. It requires two-factor authentication, such as a mobile PIN and biometric authentication (fingerprint or iris scan), to complete the transaction. Two-factor authentication UPI is meant for larger transactions and is widely used for merchant transactions.

In addition to the two types of UPI, there are also several UPI-based apps available in India, each with its own unique features and benefits. Some of the popular UPI-based apps in India include Google Pay, PhonePe, Paytm, and BHIM (Bharat Interface for Money).

Overall, UPI has become a popular and convenient way to make digital payments in India, and has played a key role in promoting financial inclusion and digitalization of the economy.

India has a well-developed banking system with a range of public sector, private sector, foreign, cooperative, and regional rural banks. The Reserve Bank of India (RBI) is the central bank of the country, and is responsible for regulating and supervising the banking system.

Some of the different types of banks in India include:

1. Public Sector Banks (PSBs): These banks are owned and operated by the government of India. They account for the majority of the banking sector in terms of assets and branches. Some of the largest PSBs in India include State Bank of India, Punjab National Bank, and Bank of Baroda.
2. Private Sector Banks: These banks are owned and operated by private entities. They have gained significant market share in recent years and are known for their modern banking practices and customer-centric approach. Some of the largest private sector banks in India include HDFC Bank, ICICI Bank, and Axis Bank.
3. Foreign Banks: These are banks that are headquartered in foreign countries but have a presence in India. They offer a range of banking services, including corporate banking, trade finance, and foreign exchange services. Some of the largest foreign banks in India include Citibank, Standard Chartered Bank, and HSBC.
4. Cooperative Banks: These are banks that are owned and operated by cooperatives, which are groups of people who come together to provide financial services to their members. Cooperative banks are typically smaller than other types of banks and are focused on serving specific communities or regions.
5. Regional Rural Banks (RRBs): These banks were established with the aim of providing banking services to rural areas in India. RRBs are jointly owned by the central government, state governments, and sponsor banks. They are primarily focused on providing credit to small and marginal farmers, artisans, and other rural entrepreneurs.

Overall, the banking sector in India is highly competitive and diverse, with a range of players catering to different segments of the market.

1. What is inflation?

a) An increase in the value of money
b) A decrease in the value of money
c) A stable value of money
d) None of the above

1. Which of the following is an example of demand-pull inflation?

a) An increase in the price of oil
b) An increase in government spending
c) An increase in the money supply
d) None of the above

3. Which of the following is an example of cost-push inflation?

a) An increase in government spending
b) A decrease in the price of oil
c) An increase in the minimum wage
d) None of the above

4. What is the most common measure of inflation?

a) Consumer Price Index (CPI)
b) Gross Domestic Product (GDP)
c) Producer Price Index (PPI)
d) None of the above

5. Which of the following is a tool of monetary policy used to control inflation?

a) Interest rates
b) Government spending
c) Taxation
d) None of the above

6. Which of the following is a tool of fiscal policy used to control inflation

a) Interest rates
b) Government spending

c) Taxation
d) None of the above

7. Which of the following is a way that banks create money?

a) By printing currency
b) By making loans
c) By collecting taxes
d) None of the above

8. What is the central bank of India?

a) State Bank of India
b) Reserve Bank of India
c) Punjab National Bank
d) HDFC Bank

9. Which of the following is a tool of monetary policy used by the Reserve Bank of India?

a) Fiscal policy
b) Interest rates
c) Government spending
d) None of the above

10. Which of the following is a type of bank in India?

a) Public sector bank
b) Private sector bank
c) Foreign bank
d) All of the above

11. Which of the following is an example of a public sector bank in India?

a) HDFC Bank
b) ICICI Bank
c) State Bank of India
d) None of the above

12. Which of the following is an example of a private sector bank in India?

    a) State Bank of India
    b) Punjab National Bank
    c) HDFC Bank
    d) None of the above

13. Which of the following is an example of a foreign bank in India?

    a) Citibank
    b) State Bank of India
    c) HDFC Bank
    d) None of the above

14. What is the full form of UPI?

    a) Universal Payment Interface
    b) United Payment Interface
    c) Unique Payment Interface
    d) None of the above

15. Which of the following is a popular UPI-based app in India?

    a) Google Pay
    b) PhonePe
    c) Paytm
    d) All of the above

CHAPTER FOUR

Indian economy

Indian Economy This chapter will cover the Indian economy's key features, including GDP, sectors of the economy, demographic trends, and key economic policies.

India is one of the fastest-growing economies in the world and has emerged as a major player in the global economy. Here are some of the key features of the Indian economy:

1. GDP: India is currently the 6th largest economy in the world with a GDP of $2.8 trillion (2020). The Indian economy has been growing at an average rate of 7% over the last decade.
2. Sectors: The Indian economy is divided into three major sectors – agriculture, industry, and services. Agriculture contributes about 18% to the GDP, industry contributes about 30%, and services contribute about 52%.
3. Labor force: India has a large labor force of about 500 million people, with about 48% of the workforce engaged in agriculture, 20% in industry, and 32% in services.
4. Foreign trade: India is one of the world's largest exporters of goods and services. Its major export items include petroleum products, gems and jewelry, textiles, and engineering goods.
5. FDI: India has been one of the fastest-growing recipients of foreign direct investment (FDI) in recent years. In 2020, India received $64 billion in FDI, making it the fifth-largest recipient of FDI in the world.
6. Infrastructure: India has made significant progress in building its infrastructure over the last few decades. The country has a vast network of roads, railways, airports, and ports, and has been investing heavily in building new infrastructure.

7. Demographics: India has a young population, with about 65% of the population below the age of 35. This demographic dividend presents a huge opportunity for the Indian economy, as young people are more likely to be productive and innovative.

8. Challenges: Despite the progress made, the Indian economy still faces several challenges, including high levels of poverty, income inequality, and unemployment. The country also faces environmental challenges, such as air and water pollution, and climate change.

Overall, the Indian economy has made significant progress in recent years and has emerged as a major player in the global economy. However, there is still a long way to go, and the country will need to address its challenges if it is to achieve sustained and inclusive growth.

The Indian economic reforms of 1991, also known as the LPG reforms, were a major turning point in the country's economic history. For decades before the reforms, India had pursued a model of socialist-style economic development, with a large public sector and numerous regulations and restrictions on private enterprise. This approach had limited success in promoting economic growth and development, and by the late 1980s, India was facing a serious economic crisis, with high inflation, a large fiscal deficit, and a balance of payments crisis.

In response to these challenges, the government of India, led by then-Prime Minister P.V. Narasimha Rao and his Finance Minister, Dr. Manmohan Singh, implemented a series of economic reforms in 1991. The reforms were aimed at creating a more open and competitive economy, with greater participation by the private sector and foreign investors. The reforms were based on three key principles: liberalization, privatization, and globalization, which became known as the LPG model.

Liberalization involved removing many of the restrictions on private enterprise that had been in place in India for decades. This included eliminating licensing requirements for many industries, allowing private companies to enter sectors that had previously been reserved for the public sector, and reducing or eliminating price controls on many goods and services.

Privatization involved selling off many of the state-owned enterprises and public sector units that had been established by the government in the years since India gained independence. These companies were often inefficient and burdened with debt, and the government believed that selling them to private investors would improve their performance and reduce the burden on the government.

Globalization involved opening up the Indian economy to greater trade and investment from other countries. This included reducing tariffs on imports and exports, allowing foreign companies to invest in many sectors of the Indian economy, and signing agreements with other countries to promote trade and investment.

The reforms had a significant impact on the Indian economy. In the years following the reforms, India's GDP growth rate increased significantly, from around 3-4% in the 1980s to an average of 6-7% in the 1990s and 2000s. Foreign investment increased, and many sectors of the economy, such as information technology and services, experienced rapid growth.

However, the reforms also had some negative consequences. They led to increased income inequality, as some sectors and regions of the country benefited more than others from the reforms. They also led to job insecurity for many workers in the public sector, as many state-owned enterprises were sold off or restructured. Additionally, some sectors, such as agriculture, were left behind by the reforms, and there were concerns about the environmental impact of increased economic activity.

Despite these challenges, the LPG reforms of 1991 marked a major turning point in the Indian economy. They laid the groundwork for the growth and development that India has experienced in the years since. The reforms opened up new opportunities for private enterprise and foreign investment, which helped to drive economic growth and create new jobs. They also helped to modernize the Indian economy, making it more efficient and globally competitive.

The LPG reforms of 1991 were not without their critics, however. Some argued that the reforms were too focused on promoting economic growth at the expense of social and environmental concerns. Others argued that the reforms did not go far enough in promoting greater social and economic equality in India.

Despite these criticisms, it is clear that the LPG reforms of 1991 marked a major turning point in the history of the Indian economy. They helped to modernize and open up the economy, laying the groundwork for the growth and development that India has experienced in the years since.

The demographic transition theory is a model that explains how populations change over time, particularly in relation to their birth and death rates. The theory suggests that populations go through a predictable sequence of changes as they move from high birth and death rates to low birth and death rates. The theory was first proposed by Frank W. Notestein in 1945 and has since been refined and expanded upon by demographers and other social scientists.

The demographic transition theory is based on the idea that changes in economic and social conditions can have a significant impact on population growth. As countries develop and become more industrialized, their birth and death rates tend to decline. This is due to a combination of factors, including improvements in public health, increased access to education and family planning, and changes in cultural attitudes towards childbearing.

The demographic transition theory is typically divided into four stages, each of which is characterized by different patterns of population growth. The first stage is the pre-industrial stage, in which birth and death rates are both high and the population grows slowly, if at all. This stage is common in many developing countries where access to modern healthcare and family planning is limited.

The second stage is the transitional stage, in which death rates begin to decline due to improvements in healthcare and living conditions. Birth rates remain high, however, resulting in rapid population growth. This stage is characterized by a demographic boom and is typically associated with the early stages of industrialization.

The third stage is the industrial stage, in which both birth and death rates decline as a result of increased access to education, family planning, and other social and economic factors. This stage is characterized by slower population growth and is common in many developed countries.

The fourth stage is the post-industrial stage, in which birth and death rates are both low and the population grows slowly, if at all. This stage is typically associated with developed countries where birth rates have fallen below the replacement level.

It is important to note that the demographic transition theory is not without its critics. Some scholars have argued that the theory oversimplifies the complex social and economic factors that influence population growth, and that it does not adequately account for cultural and political differences between countries. Others have suggested that the theory is too focused on changes in birth and death rates, and that it does not fully consider other factors that can impact population growth, such as migration patterns and changes in household size.

Despite these criticisms, the demographic transition theory remains a useful framework for understanding the ways in which populations change over time. By examining the social and economic factors that influence population growth, demographers and other social scientists can gain insights into the challenges and opportunities facing countries as they navigate the process of demographic change. These insights can help policymakers develop strategies for addressing issues such as population aging, workforce development, and social welfare.

India's demographic transition has been a subject of great interest and scrutiny for many years. Like many other countries, India has undergone significant changes in its population growth and structure over the past few decades. These changes have been driven by a variety of social, economic, and cultural factors, and have had important implications for the country's development.

India's demographic transition began in the mid-20th century, as the country experienced improvements in healthcare and living conditions. During this time, the death rate began to decline, while the birth rate remained high. This led to a rapid increase in the population, which more than doubled between 1951 and 2001.

However, in recent years, India's demographic transition has entered a new phase, as birth rates have begun to decline. This decline is due in part to improvements in access to education and family planning services, as well as changes in cultural attitudes towards childbearing. As a result, India's population growth has slowed significantly, from a peak of 2.2% per year in the 1970s to around 1.2% per year in the 2010s.

One of the key implications of India's demographic transition is the changing age structure of its population. As birth rates decline and people live longer, the proportion of older adults in the population is increasing. This trend is likely to continue in the coming decades, as India's fertility rate is projected to continue declining and life expectancy is projected to continue increasing.

The aging of India's population has important implications for the country's development. As the proportion of older adults in the population increases, there will be greater demand for healthcare, social welfare, and other services that are typically associated with aging populations. At the same time, the proportion of working-age adults in the population may decline, which could have implications for economic growth and development.

To address these challenges, policymakers in India will need to develop strategies for promoting sustainable population growth and addressing the needs of older adults. This may involve investing in healthcare and social welfare programs, improving access to education and family planning services, and promoting policies that support workforce development and economic growth.

Overall, India's demographic transition is a complex and ongoing process that has important implications for the country's future. By understanding the social, economic, and cultural factors that are driving these changes, policymakers can develop strategies that support sustainable development and address the challenges and opportunities of an aging population.

Demographic dividend is a term used to describe the potential economic benefits that arise from a demographic shift in the age structure of a population. It occurs when the working-age population (between 15 and 64 years of age) grows faster than the dependent population (those under 15 years of age and over 65 years of age). India is currently experiencing a demographic dividend, and it is expected to continue until 2040.

India's demographic dividend can be attributed to several factors, including a decline in fertility rates, improvements in healthcare and sanitation, and an increase in education levels. These factors have led to a significant increase in the working-age population in recent years, which is expected to peak in the next few decades.

The demographic dividend presents a significant opportunity for India to accelerate its economic growth and development. With a large and growing workforce, India has the potential to become a major economic power in the coming years. However, realizing this potential will require significant investments in education, healthcare, and infrastructure, as well as policies that promote economic growth and job creation.

One of the key challenges that India faces in realizing its demographic dividend is ensuring that the workforce is adequately trained and educated to take advantage of the opportunities that arise. While India has made significant progress in improving access to education in recent years, there is still a significant skills gap that needs to be addressed. This will require investments in vocational training and higher education, as well as policies that promote innovation and entrepreneurship.

Another challenge that India faces in realizing its demographic dividend is addressing the needs of the growing elderly population. While the working-age population is growing, the proportion of elderly people is also increasing, which presents significant challenges for healthcare, social welfare, and other services. Addressing these challenges will require significant investments in healthcare and social welfare programs, as well as policies that promote healthy aging.

In conclusion, India's demographic dividend presents a significant opportunity for economic growth and development. However, realizing this potential will require significant investments in education, healthcare, and infrastructure, as well as policies that promote economic growth and job creation. By addressing these challenges and taking advantage of the opportunities that arise, India can become a major economic power in the coming years.

Globalization has had a significant impact on the Indian economy. Here are some of the key effects:

1. Increased Foreign Investment: Globalization has led to a significant increase in foreign investment in India. This has resulted in the growth of various sectors such as manufacturing, services, and infrastructure. Foreign investment has also brought in new technology and expertise, which has helped in improving the overall competitiveness of Indian industries.

2. Increased Exports: Globalization has provided Indian companies with access to larger markets, resulting in increased exports. This has helped in improving the balance of trade, and has contributed to the growth of the Indian economy.

3. Job Creation: The growth of various sectors as a result of globalization has created new job opportunities in India. However, it has also resulted in the displacement of workers from traditional industries.

4. Increase in GDP: The Indian economy has grown significantly in the last few decades due to globalization. This has resulted in an increase in the GDP of the country.

5. Changes in Agriculture: Globalization has resulted in a shift in Indian agriculture from traditional crops to cash crops. This has led to an increase in exports, but has also resulted in the neglect of traditional crops.

6. Income Inequality: While globalization has brought economic growth to India, it has also resulted in income inequality. The benefits of globalization have been unevenly distributed, with some segments of

society benefiting more than others.

Overall, globalization has had a mixed impact on the Indian economy, with both positive and negative effects.

1. Which industry contributes the most to the Indian economy?

    a) Agriculture
    b) Manufacturing
    c) Services
    d) Mining

1. Which of the following sectors in India has seen the most foreign investment in recent years

    a) Agriculture
    b) Manufacturing
    c) Services
    d) Retail

3. What is the current GDP growth rate of India?

    a) 2%
    b) 4%
    c) 6%
    d) 8%

4. Which of the following is the largest employer in India?

    a) Agriculture
    b) Manufacturing
    c) Services
    d) Mining

5. What is the current inflation rate in India

    a) 2%
    b) 4%

c) 6%
d) 8%

6. Which of the following industries is considered the backbone of the Indian economy? a) Agriculture

   b) Manufacturing
   c) Services
   d) Retail

7. Which of the following is the largest export item from India?

   a) Textiles
   b) Pharmaceuticals
   c) Software
   d) Automobiles

8. What is the primary source of tax revenue for the Indian government?

   a) Corporate taxes
   b) Income taxes
   c) Sales taxes
   d) Excise taxes

9. What is the main factor driving India's population growth?

   a) High birth rate
   b) High immigration
   c) High life expectancy
   d) High fertility rate

10. Which of the following sectors is responsible for the highest percentage of employment in India?

    a) Agriculture
    b) Manufacturing
    c) Services
    d) Mining

11. Which of the following industries has the highest GDP contribution in India?

    a) Agriculture
    b) Manufacturing
    c) Services
    d) Mining

12. What is the current poverty rate in India?

    a) 10%
    b) 20%
    c) 30%
    d) 40%

13. Which of the following is not a major stock exchange in India?

    a) BSE
    b) NSE
    c) NYSE
    d) MSEI

14. What is the largest public sector bank in India?

    a) State Bank of India
    b) Punjab National Bank
    c) Bank of Baroda
    d) Canara Bank

15. What is the name of the Indian currency?

    a) Rupee
    b) Rupiah
    c) Ringgit
    d) Renminbi

CHAPTER FIVE

International trade

International trade refers to the exchange of goods and services between countries. It involves the buying and selling of goods and services across international borders, often through the use of trade agreements and treaties that promote open trade and free flow of goods and services.

International trade is an important aspect of the global economy, as it enables countries to access resources and products that they may not have domestically, while also allowing them to sell their own goods and services to other countries. It can also provide opportunities for businesses to expand their customer base and increase profits.

International trade can take many forms, including the import and export of goods, foreign direct investment, and the exchange of services such as tourism and consulting. It can be conducted through various channels, such as e-commerce platforms, physical marketplaces, and international trade fairs and exhibitions.

Overall, international trade plays a critical role in shaping global economic growth and development, as it enables countries to specialize in the production of goods and services that they have a comparative advantage in, leading to increased efficiency and productivity.

Trade barriers refer to any measures that restrict or impede the free flow of goods and services between countries. They can be applied by governments, organizations, or individuals, and can take many different forms.

Types of Trade Barriers:

1. Tariffs: Tariffs are taxes that are levied on imported goods, making them more expensive than domestically produced goods. This can make it difficult for foreign producers to compete with domestic producers and may lead to decreased imports and increased exports.

2. Quotas: Quotas are limits on the amount of goods that can be imported into a country. They can be used to protect domestic producers from foreign competition, but can also limit consumer choice and increase prices.

3. Embargoes: Embargoes are complete bans on the import or export of goods with a particular country or group of countries. They can be used for political or economic reasons, but can also lead to shortages and increased prices.

4. Standards and Regulations: Standards and regulations are rules and requirements that products must meet before they can be sold in a particular country. They can be used to protect consumers and the environment, but can also be used as a barrier to trade if they are overly strict or difficult to comply with.

5. Subsidies: Subsidies are financial incentives that are given to domestic producers to help them compete with foreign producers. They can distort the market and lead to overproduction and lower quality products.

6. Voluntary Export Restraints (VERs): VERs are agreements between countries where the exporting country voluntarily agrees to limit the amount of goods that it exports to a particular country. They can be used to avoid more restrictive trade measures, but can also limit consumer choice and increase prices.

Overall, trade barriers can have a significant impact on international trade and can either promote or hinder economic growth and development. While some trade barriers may be necessary to protect domestic industries or consumers, they can also limit competition, reduce efficiency, and increase costs for businesses and consumers.

Exchange rates refer to the value of one currency in relation to another. They are determined by the forces of supply and demand in the foreign exchange market, where buyers and sellers exchange one currency for another.

Exchange rates are important because they affect international trade, investment, and economic growth. Changes in exchange rates can have a significant impact on the prices of imported and exported goods, as well as on the profits of businesses that operate across borders. Exchange rates also affect the cost of international travel and tourism, as well as the returns on foreign investments.

Exchange rates can be classified into two types:

1. Fixed exchange rates: A fixed exchange rate is a system where the value of a currency is fixed to a specific value or a range of values in relation to another currency or a basket of currencies. This system is usually maintained by a central bank, which buys or sells its own currency in order to maintain the fixed exchange rate. This system provides stability in exchange rates but can limit a country's ability to adjust to changes in its economy.
2. Floating exchange rates: A floating exchange rate is a system where the value of a currency is determined by the forces of supply and demand in the foreign exchange market. The exchange rate fluctuates based on the economic conditions of the country, such as inflation, interest rates, and economic growth. This system allows for more flexibility in adjusting to changes in the economy, but can also lead to volatility in exchange rates.

Exchange rates are often quoted as the price of one currency in terms of another. For example, if the exchange rate between the US dollar and the euro is 1.2, it means that one US dollar can be exchanged for 1.2 euros. Exchange rates are constantly changing and can be affected by many factors, including economic indicators, geopolitical events, and central bank policies.

Trade agreements are formal agreements between two or more countries that govern their trading relationship. These agreements are designed to promote free and fair trade by reducing trade barriers such as tariffs, quotas, and other restrictions on imports and exports.

Trade agreements typically cover a wide range of issues related to trade, including:

1. Tariffs and duties: Tariffs are taxes imposed on imported goods, and trade agreements often seek to reduce or eliminate them. Trade agreements may also address other types of duties, such as anti-dumping duties or countervailing duties.
2. Non-tariff barriers: Non-tariff barriers are any other types of restrictions on trade, such as quotas, licensing requirements, technical standards, and other regulations. Trade agreements may seek to reduce or eliminate these barriers as well.

3. Intellectual property: Trade agreements often address issues related to intellectual property, such as patents, trademarks, and copyrights. These agreements may set standards for protecting intellectual property rights across borders.
4. Services: Many trade agreements cover trade in services, such as financial services, telecommunications, and transportation.
5. Investment: Trade agreements may also include provisions related to foreign investment, such as rules for protecting foreign investors and resolving disputes between investors and host governments.

Some of the major trade agreements in the world include:

1. World Trade Organization (WTO): The WTO is a global organization that sets rules for international trade and provides a forum for negotiating new trade agreements.
2. North American Free Trade Agreement (NAFTA): NAFTA is a trade agreement between Canada, the United States, and Mexico that eliminates most tariffs on goods traded between the three countries.
3. European Union (EU): The EU is a regional organization that promotes free trade among its member countries and has negotiated numerous trade agreements with other countries and regions.
4. Trans-Pacific Partnership (TPP): The TPP was a proposed trade agreement between 12 countries in the Asia-Pacific region, but the United States withdrew from the agreement in 2017.

Trade agreements can have both positive and negative effects on countries and their economies. Supporters of trade agreements argue that they can increase trade and investment, create jobs, and promote economic growth. Critics argue that trade agreements can lead to job losses and other negative effects on certain industries and workers, and that they can undermine environmental and labor standards.

Balance of payments (BoP) is a record of all economic transactions between residents of a country and the rest of the world over a given period of time, typically a year. It is a measure of a country's economic interactions with the rest of the world, including trade in goods and services, income flows, and capital transfers.

The BoP is divided into two main components: the current account and the capital account.

1. Current account: The current account measures a country's trade in goods and services, income flows, and unilateral transfers. It includes exports and imports of goods and services, as well as income received from investments abroad and payments made to foreign investors. Unilateral transfers include gifts, grants, and other transfers that do not involve a direct exchange of goods or services.

2. Capital account: The capital account measures the flow of capital into and out of a country, including foreign investment, portfolio investment, and changes in foreign exchange reserves. It includes both inflows and outflows of capital, and reflects the net change in a country's foreign assets and liabilities.

If a country is running a current account surplus, it means that it is exporting more goods and services than it is importing, and is receiving more income from investments abroad than it is paying out. This can indicate a strong export sector and a favorable balance of trade. On the other hand, if a country is running a current account deficit, it means that it is importing more goods and services than it is exporting, and is paying out more income to foreign investors than it is receiving. This can indicate a weak export sector and a reliance on foreign investment.

Similarly, if a country is running a capital account surplus, it means that it is receiving more capital inflows than outflows, and is accumulating foreign assets. This can indicate investor confidence in the country's economy and financial system. Conversely, if a country is running a capital account deficit, it means that it is experiencing more capital outflows than inflows, and is depleting its foreign assets. This can indicate a lack of investor confidence or a need to finance a current account deficit.

In summary, the balance of payments is an important measure of a country's economic interactions with the rest of the world, and can provide insight into its trade relationships, investment flows, and overall economic performance.

The international monetary system refers to the framework of rules, institutions, and procedures that govern the exchange of currencies and other financial assets between countries. It is a complex system that affects the global economy, financial markets, and individual countries.

The international monetary system has evolved over time, with several key milestones that have shaped its development. These include:

1. The gold standard: The gold standard was a monetary system that was widely used in the 19th and early 20th centuries. Under this system, currencies were backed by gold, and countries agreed to exchange their currencies for gold at a fixed rate.

2. The Bretton Woods system: The Bretton Woods system was established in 1944 after World War II to stabilize the global economy. It was based on the US dollar as the world's reserve currency, which was backed by gold. Under this system, other countries fixed their exchange rates to the US dollar, and the International Monetary Fund (IMF) was created to oversee the system.

3. The floating exchange rate system: In the early 1970s, the Bretton Woods system broke down as the US ended the convertibility of the dollar to gold. This led to the development of the floating exchange rate system, in which exchange rates are determined by supply and demand in the foreign exchange market.

4. The Eurozone: The Eurozone is a monetary union consisting of 19 European Union (EU) member states that have adopted the euro as their common currency. The Eurozone is governed by the European Central Bank (ECB), which is responsible for monetary policy and maintaining the stability of the euro.

Today, the international monetary system is characterized by a mix of fixed and floating exchange rates, with some countries using the US dollar or euro as their reserve currency. The IMF continues to play a key role in promoting international monetary cooperation and maintaining global financial stability.

The international monetary system is subject to a number of challenges and risks, including currency fluctuations, trade imbalances, and financial crises. As a result, policymakers and financial institutions must work together to manage these risks and maintain the stability of the global financial system.

1. Which of the following is a characteristic of international trade?

    a. It refers to the exchange of goods and services within a country.
    b. It involves only the export of goods and services.
    c. It involves the exchange of goods and services between countries.

d. It involves the exchange of goods and services between individuals within a country.

Answer: c. It involves the exchange of goods and services between countries.

1. Which of the following is a trade barrier?

a. Import quota
b. Free trade agreement
c. Balance of payments
d. Exchange rate
Answer: a. Import quota

3. Which type of trade barrier involves the imposition of taxes on imports?

a. Import quota
b. Tariff
c. Embargo
d. Subsidy
Answer: b. Tariff

4. What was the Bretton Woods agreement?

a. An agreement to establish a gold standard for international trade
b. An agreement to establish a fixed exchange rate system
c. An agreement to establish a free trade system
d. An agreement to establish a currency union
Answer: b. An agreement to establish a fixed exchange rate system

5. What was the role of the US dollar in the Bretton Woods system?

a. It was the world's reserve currency.
b. It was backed by gold.
c. It was the only currency that could be used for international trade.
d. It was pegged to the price of gold.
Answer: a. It was the world's reserve currency.

6. Which organization was established to oversee the Bretton Woods system?

   a. International Monetary Fund (IMF)
   b. World Trade Organization (WTO)
   c. World Bank d. United Nations (UN)
   Answer: a. International Monetary Fund (IMF)

7. Which country was the primary driver behind the creation of the Bretton Woods system?

   a. Germany
   b. Japan
   c. United Kingdom
   d. United States
   Answer: d. United States

8. What was the key feature of the Bretton Woods system?

   a. Fixed exchange rates
   b. Floating exchange rates
   c. Free trade
   d. Gold standard
   Answer: a. Fixed exchange rates

9. Which of the following is a challenge of the Bretton Woods system?

   a. Currency fluctuations
   b. Free trade
   c. Flexible exchange
   d. Floating exchange rates
   Answer: a. Currency fluctuations

10. What led to the collapse of the Bretton Woods system?

    a. The US ending the convertibility of the dollar to gold
    b. The adoption of the euro by European countries
    c. The creation of the World Trade Organization (WTO)

d. The devaluation of the Japanese yen
Answer: a. The US ending the convertibility of the dollar to gold

11. Which country was the first to abandon the Bretton Woods system

   a. Germany
   b. Japan
   c. United Kingdom
   d. United States
   Answer: d. United States

12. What is the primary goal of the International Monetary Fund (IMF)?

   a. To promote free trade
   b. To maintain stable exchange rates
   c. To establish a gold standard
   d. To create a currency union
   Answer: b. To maintain stable exchange rates

CHAPTER SIX

Budget

A budget is a financial plan that estimates the income and expenditure for a specific period of time. It is an important tool for financial planning and control, as it helps individuals, businesses, and governments to manage their finances effectively.

There are several types of budgets, including:

1. Personal budget: This is a budget created by an individual or a household to manage their personal finances, including income, expenses, and savings.
2. Business budget: This is a budget created by a business or organization to manage its finances, including revenues, expenses, and profits.
3. Operating budget: This is a budget that outlines the income and expenses for a specific period, usually a year, and is used to guide day-to-day operations.
4. Capital budget: This is a budget that outlines the planned investments in long-term assets, such as property, equipment, or infrastructure.
5. Cash budget: This is a budget that focuses on the inflows and outflows of cash, providing a detailed analysis of the cash position of an individual, business, or government.
6. Project budget: This is a budget that is created for a specific project or initiative, outlining the costs and expected returns.
7. National budget: This is a budget created by the government to manage its finances, including revenue collection, expenditure, and debt management. The national budget is a key tool for fiscal policy and economic management.

1. The history of budgets in India can be traced back to the colonial era, when the British government established a system of financial

management for the country. The first budget in India was presented in 1860 by James Wilson, who was then the Finance Member of the Indian Council.

2. During the colonial period, the Indian budget was primarily focused on raising revenue for the British government, rather than on promoting economic development or social welfare. The budget was largely based on the "Indian Budget Statement," which was an annual report on the financial position of the country.

3. After independence in 1947, the Indian government established the Planning Commission to develop a comprehensive economic plan for the country. The Planning Commission worked closely with the Finance Ministry to develop the annual budget, which became an important tool for economic planning and development.

4. In the early years of independence, the Indian budget was focused on developing basic infrastructure and industries, such as agriculture, transportation, and manufacturing. The government also introduced a range of social welfare programs, such as food subsidies and rural employment schemes, to alleviate poverty and promote social equity.

5. However, the Indian economy faced a range of challenges in the 1960s and 1970s, including high inflation, low growth, and a balance of payments crisis. In response, the government introduced a range of economic reforms, including devaluation of the currency, import substitution policies, and nationalization of key industries.

6. During this period, the Indian budget became increasingly focused on fiscal discipline and deficit reduction, with a range of measures introduced to control government spending and increase revenue collection. The government also introduced a range of tax incentives to promote investment and economic growth.

7. In the 1990s, India began to liberalize its economy, opening up to foreign investment and trade. This led to significant changes in the budget, with a greater emphasis on fiscal discipline, market-oriented reforms, and social welfare programs. The government also introduced a range of measures to improve infrastructure, such as highways and airports, and to promote the growth of the services sector, including IT and tourism.

8. In recent years, the Indian budget has been focused on promoting inclusive growth and development, with a particular emphasis on improving infrastructure, healthcare, education, and social welfare programs. The budget also includes measures to promote

entrepreneurship and innovation, such as tax incentives and funding for start-ups.

9. Overall, the Indian budget has played a crucial role in shaping the country's economic development over the past century, and it continues to be an important tool for fiscal policy and economic management. The budget has evolved over time in response to changing economic conditions and priorities, reflecting the complex interplay between economic, social, and political factors in shaping the country's economic trajectory.

The Union Budget of India is an annual financial statement presented by the Finance Minister of India to the Parliament. It is a comprehensive document that outlines the government's revenue and expenditure for the upcoming financial year, and includes a range of policy measures and proposals aimed at promoting economic growth, job creation, and social welfare.

The Union Budget is divided into two parts: the Revenue Budget and the Capital Budget. The Revenue Budget includes the government's revenue receipts and expenditures, while the Capital Budget includes capital receipts and expenditures.

The Revenue Budget is further divided into two parts: the Plan Revenue Expenditure and the Non-Plan Revenue Expenditure. The Plan Revenue Expenditure includes all expenses related to planned economic development, while the Non-Plan Revenue Expenditure includes all other expenses such as interest payments, subsidies, and defense expenditures.

The Capital Budget includes items such as loans raised by the government, investments in public sector enterprises, and other capital receipts. It is further divided into two parts: the Plan Capital Expenditure and the Non-Plan Capital Expenditure. The Plan Capital Expenditure includes all expenses related to planned economic development, while the Non-Plan Capital Expenditure includes all other capital expenses such as investment in public sector enterprises.

The Union Budget also includes a range of policy measures and proposals aimed at promoting economic growth, job creation, and social welfare. These measures may include changes to tax rates, incentives for investment and innovation, and funding for key sectors such as agriculture, healthcare, education, and infrastructure.

The process of preparing the Union Budget typically begins in December or January of each year, when various departments and ministries submit their proposals for funding to the Finance Ministry. The Finance Ministry then prepares a draft budget, which is reviewed and approved by the Cabinet before being presented to the Parliament in late February or early March.

The presentation of the Union Budget is a highly anticipated event in India, with extensive media coverage and public scrutiny of the government's proposals. The budget is also closely watched by investors and businesses, as it can have a significant impact on the economy and financial markets.

One of the key objectives of the Union Budget is to promote economic growth and development. To achieve this, the budget may include a range of measures aimed at stimulating investment and innovation, such as tax incentives and funding for research and development.

The budget may also include measures to support specific sectors of the economy, such as agriculture, healthcare, and education. For example, the government may allocate funds for improving irrigation facilities in rural areas, or for constructing new schools and hospitals.

In addition to promoting economic growth, the Union Budget also plays an important role in promoting social welfare. The budget may include measures aimed at reducing poverty and inequality, such as food subsidies, rural employment schemes, and social security programs.

The budget may also include measures aimed at improving access to education and healthcare, such as funding for new schools and hospitals, and subsidies for medical treatment and medicines.

Overall, the Union Budget is a critical tool for the Indian government in managing the country's finances and promoting economic development. Its annual presentation reflects the government's priorities and policies, and its implementation can have far-reaching consequences for the country's economic growth and social welfare.

The history of the Union Budget in India dates back to the colonial era, when the British government established a system of financial management for the country. The first budget in India was presented in 1860 by James Wilson, who was then the Finance Member of the Indian Council.

During the colonial period, the Indian budget was primarily focused on raising revenue for the British government, rather than on promoting economic development or social welfare. The budget was largely based on the "Indian Budget Statement," which was an annual report on the financial position of the country.

1. Who presents the Union Budget in India?

   a) The President of India
   b) The Prime Minister of India
   c) The Finance Minister of India
   d) The Chief Economic Advisor

1. When is the Union Budget presented in India?

   a) In December
   b) In January
   c) In February or March
   d) In April

3. Which of the following is not a part of the Union Budget?

   a) The Revenue Budget
   b) The Capital Budget
   c) The Social Welfare Budget
   d) The Plan Budget

4. What is the primary objective of the Union Budget?

   a) To promote economic growth and development
   b) To reduce poverty and inequality
   c) To increase social welfare
   d) To reduce the fiscal deficit

5. What is the history of the Union Budget in India?

   a) It dates back to the colonial era
   b) It was established in 1947 after independence
   c) It was first presented in 1950 after the adoption of the Constitution
   d) It was introduced in 1991 as part of economic liberalization

6. Which of the following is not a component of the Revenue Budget?

    a) Plan Revenue Expenditure
    b) Non-Plan Revenue Expenditure
    c) Plan Capital Expenditure
    d) Non-Plan Capital Expenditure

7. Which of the following is not a component of the Capital Budget?

    a) Loans raised by the government
    b) Investment in public sector enterprises
    c) Plan Capital Expenditure
    d) Non-Plan Capital Expenditure

8. What is the difference between the Plan and Non-Plan Budget?

    a) The Plan Budget is focused on economic development, while the Non-Plan Budget includes all other expenses
    b) The Plan Budget includes all expenses related to planned economic development, while the Non-Plan Budget includes all other expenses
    c) The Plan Budget is prepared by the Planning Commission, while the Non-Plan Budget is prepared by the Finance Ministry
    d) The Plan Budget is presented separately from the Non-Plan Budget

9. Which of the following is not a policy measure that may be included in the Union Budget?

    a) Tax incentives
    b) Funding for research and development
    c) Funding for new sports stadiums
    d) Investment in infrastructure

10. Which of the following is not a sector that may receive funding from the Union Budget?

    a) Agriculture
    b) Healthcare
    c) Education

d) Telecommunications

11. What is the role of the Union Budget in promoting social welfare?

a) It may include measures aimed at reducing poverty and inequality
b) It may include measures aimed at improving access to education and healthcare c) It may include measures aimed at providing social security programs
d) All of the above

12. How is the Union Budget prepared?

a) Various departments and ministries submit their proposals for funding to the Planning Commission
b) Various departments and ministries submit their proposals for funding to the Finance Ministry
c) The President of India prepares the budget in consultation with the Prime Minister d) The Chief Economic Advisor prepares the budget in consultation with the Finance Minister

13. When was the first budget presented in India?

a) In 1860
b) In 1947
c) In 1950
d) In 1991

14. What was the focus of the Indian budget during the colonial period?

a) Promoting economic development and social welfare
b) Raising revenue for the British government
c) Providing social security programs
d) Investing in infrastructure

15. Who presented the first budget in India?

a) Jawaharlal Nehru
b) Indira Gandhi

c) James Wilson
d) Sard

CHAPTER SEVEN

Economic Organizations

The World Trade Organization (WTO) is an intergovernmental organization that regulates and promotes international trade. It was established on January 1, 1995, after the Uruguay Round of negotiations, which took place from 1986 to 1994. The WTO replaced the General Agreement on Tariffs and Trade (GATT), which was established after World War II to reduce tariffs and promote international trade.

The WTO has 164 member countries, and its headquarters is located in Geneva, Switzerland. The organization is based on the principle of non-discrimination, meaning that member countries should not discriminate between their trading partners. The WTO also promotes the free flow of goods, services, and capital across borders.

The main objectives of the WTO are to promote economic growth and development, reduce poverty, and create jobs by facilitating international trade. It does this by providing a platform for negotiations between member countries to reduce trade barriers, such as tariffs and quotas. The WTO also provides a forum for resolving disputes between member countries related to trade.

One of the key functions of the WTO is to monitor and enforce the trade agreements that it oversees. The organization has a dispute settlement mechanism that allows member countries to resolve disputes through a neutral and binding process. This mechanism has been used successfully to resolve many disputes between member countries, including those related to agricultural subsidies, intellectual property rights, and trade in services.

The WTO also provides technical assistance and training to developing countries to help them participate more fully in the global trading system. This includes support for building capacity in areas such as trade policy, trade facilitation, and customs procedures. The WTO also works to ensure that the interests of developing countries are taken into account in trade negotiations.

The WTO has been criticized for various reasons. Some critics argue that the organization is too focused on promoting the interests of developed countries, and that its rules and regulations are too restrictive for developing countries. Others argue that the organization does not do enough to promote environmental and social standards in international trade.

Despite these criticisms, the WTO has been successful in promoting international trade and reducing trade barriers. Since its establishment, global trade has grown significantly, and the WTO has played a key role in this growth. The organization has also helped to create a more predictable and stable international trading system, which has benefited both developed and developing countries.

In conclusion, the World Trade Organization is an important international organization that plays a crucial role in regulating and promoting international trade. It has been successful in reducing trade barriers, resolving disputes between member countries, and promoting economic growth and development. While there are criticisms of the WTO, its achievements cannot be overlooked, and the organization remains an important forum for international trade negotiations and dispute resolution.

The International Monetary Fund (IMF) is an international organization that promotes international monetary cooperation, facilitates international trade, promotes economic growth, and helps to reduce poverty around the world. It was established in 1944, along with the World Bank, as part of the Bretton Woods Agreement.

The IMF has 190 member countries, and its headquarters is located in Washington, D.C. The organization is responsible for overseeing the international monetary system, which includes exchange rate policies, international payments, and the balance of payments. The IMF also provides loans and technical assistance to member countries to help them address balance of payments problems and other economic challenges.

One of the main functions of the IMF is to provide loans to member countries that are experiencing balance of payments difficulties. These loans are typically provided with conditions attached, such as requirements for economic reform and policy changes. The IMF also provides technical assistance to member countries to help them implement economic reforms and strengthen their economic institutions.

Another key function of the IMF is to provide surveillance and monitoring of member countries' economic policies. The organization conducts regular reviews of member countries' economic policies and provides recommendations for policy changes as needed. This helps to promote economic stability and prevent financial crises.

The IMF has been criticized for various reasons. Some critics argue that the organization is too focused on promoting neoliberal economic policies, which can be harmful to developing countries. Others argue that the organization has not done enough to address issues such as income inequality and environmental degradation.

Despite these criticisms, the IMF has been successful in promoting economic growth and stability around the world. Its loans and technical assistance have helped many countries to address economic challenges and achieve sustained economic growth. The organization's monitoring and surveillance activities have also helped to prevent financial crises and promote international economic stability.

In conclusion, the International Monetary Fund is an important international organization that plays a key role in promoting international monetary cooperation, facilitating international trade, and promoting economic growth and stability. While there are criticisms of the organization, its achievements cannot be overlooked, and it remains an important institution for promoting economic development and stability around the world.

The World Trade Organization (WTO) is an international organization that was established in 1995 to promote free trade and facilitate international economic cooperation. It has 164 member countries, and its headquarters is located in Geneva, Switzerland.

The main goal of the WTO is to promote free trade by reducing barriers to international trade and promoting fair competition. The organization provides a forum for member countries to negotiate and agree on trade rules and policies. It also provides a dispute resolution mechanism to resolve trade disputes between member countries.

One of the key functions of the WTO is to oversee and enforce the General Agreement on Tariffs and Trade (GATT), which was established in 1947. The GATT is a set of rules and principles that govern international trade, including rules on tariffs, non-tariff barriers, and trade in services. The WTO has expanded on the GATT by adding new agreements on areas such as intellectual property rights, services trade, and investment.

The WTO also provides technical assistance and training to developing countries to help them participate more effectively in the global trading system. This includes assistance with trade negotiations, building trade-related infrastructure, and improving trade facilitation measures.

The WTO has been criticized by some for various reasons. Some critics argue that the organization promotes free trade at the expense of developing countries, while others argue that it does not do enough to promote environmental and labor standards. The organization has also faced criticism for its dispute resolution mechanism, which some argue is biased in favor of developed countries.

Despite these criticisms, the WTO has been successful in promoting free trade and facilitating international economic cooperation. The organization has helped to reduce tariffs and other trade barriers around the world, which has led to increased trade and economic growth. It has also provided a forum for member countries to negotiate and agree on trade rules, which has helped to promote a more stable and predictable global trading system.

In conclusion, the World Trade Organization is an important international organization that plays a key role in promoting free trade and facilitating international economic cooperation. While there are criticisms of the organization, its achievements cannot be overlooked, and it remains an important institution for promoting economic development and stability around the world.

The World Bank is an international financial institution that was established in 1944 with the goal of reducing poverty and promoting economic development in low- and middle-income countries. It is headquartered in Washington, D.C. and currently has 189 member countries.

The World Bank provides loans, grants, and technical assistance to developing countries to support their economic development efforts. Its activities are focused on a wide range of sectors, including agriculture, education, energy, health, and transportation. The World Bank also provides support for economic policy and institutional reforms, as well as for the development of private sector industries.

One of the key roles of the World Bank is to provide financial assistance to developing countries. The Bank provides loans to support specific projects or programs, as well as policy-based loans to support economic policy reforms. It also provides grants to support social programs and investments in areas such as health and education.

In addition to financial assistance, the World Bank provides technical assistance and advisory services to help countries build the capacity needed to implement development programs and policies. This includes support for institutional reforms, training and education programs, and knowledge sharing and dissemination.

The World Bank has been criticized by some for various reasons. Some argue that the institution promotes a neoliberal economic agenda that prioritizes free-market policies and economic liberalization over social and environmental concerns. Others argue that the World Bank's lending practices have contributed to debt burdens in developing countries, and that its policies have led to negative social and environmental impacts.

Despite these criticisms, the World Bank has played a key role in promoting economic development and reducing poverty around the world. Its programs have helped to improve access to education, healthcare, and other essential services, and have supported the growth of private sector industries in developing countries. While there is still much work to be done to address the root causes of poverty and inequality, the World Bank remains an important institution for promoting economic development and reducing poverty in the world's poorest countries.

In conclusion, the World Bank is a critical institution for promoting economic development and reducing poverty in developing countries. While there are valid criticisms of the institution, its achievements cannot be overlooked, and its continued support for development efforts will be critical in the years to come.

CHAPTER EIGHT

GST and Demonitization

Taxation is a critical component of any economy, as it provides the government with the necessary resources to fund public goods and services. In India, there are several different types of taxes that are levied by the central and state governments.

Direct taxes are taxes that are levied on the income or wealth of individuals or businesses. In India, the major direct taxes are income tax and wealth tax. Income tax is a tax on the income earned by individuals, while wealth tax is a tax on the wealth held by individuals, such as property or investments.

Indirect taxes are taxes that are levied on goods and services. In India, the major indirect taxes are the goods and services tax (GST), excise duty, customs duty, and value-added tax (VAT). GST is a unified tax that replaced several previous indirect taxes and is levied on the supply of goods and services across India. Excise duty is a tax on goods produced in India, while customs duty is a tax on goods imported into India. VAT is a tax on the value added at each stage of production and distribution of goods and services.

Apart from these major taxes, there are also other taxes and levies such as stamp duty, property tax, entertainment tax, and professional tax that are levied by state governments.

The Indian government has implemented several reforms in recent years to simplify the tax system and increase compliance. The introduction of GST, in particular, has been a significant reform that has helped to streamline the tax system and reduce the burden on businesses. The government has also implemented initiatives such as the Direct Benefit Transfer (DBT) scheme, which provides subsidies and benefits directly to beneficiaries through their bank accounts, to improve the efficiency and transparency of government spending.

Overall, taxation is an important aspect of the Indian economy and plays a critical role in funding public goods and services. While there have been efforts to simplify the tax system and increase compliance, there is still a need for further reforms to improve the efficiency and effectiveness of the tax system in India.

Direct taxes are taxes that are levied directly on the income or wealth of individuals or businesses. The most common example of a direct tax is income tax, which is a tax on the income earned by individuals or entities. Other examples of direct taxes include wealth tax, property tax, and estate tax.

Indirect taxes, on the other hand, are taxes that are levied on the sale or consumption of goods and services. Indirect taxes are typically included in the price of goods and services, and are therefore paid by the consumer. Examples of indirect taxes include sales tax, excise tax, customs duty, and value-added tax (VAT).

Both direct and indirect taxes play an important role in funding government programs and services, as well as regulating economic activity. The distribution of the tax burden between direct and indirect taxes can have important economic and social implications, and governments must carefully consider the design and implementation of their tax policies to ensure that they are equitable and effective.

The Goods and Services Tax (GST) is a unified tax system that was implemented in India on July 1, 2017. GST is a comprehensive tax system that replaces several previous indirect taxes, including excise duty, service tax, and value-added tax (VAT). The introduction of GST was a significant reform that aimed to streamline the tax system and reduce the compliance burden on businesses.

Under the GST system, taxes are levied on the supply of goods and services across India. GST is a consumption-based tax, meaning that it is levied on the value added at each stage of production and distribution of goods and services. This means that businesses can claim credit for the GST they have paid on inputs, which helps to reduce the overall tax burden.

There are three types of GST in India: Central GST (CGST), State GST (SGST), and Integrated GST (IGST). CGST and SGST are levied by the central and state governments, respectively, on intra-state transactions. IGST is levied on inter-state transactions and is collected by the central government, which then distributes the revenue to the relevant states.

The GST rates in India vary depending on the type of goods or services being supplied. There are four main GST rates: 5%, 12%, 18%, and 28%. There is also a zero rate for certain goods and services, such as exports and some agricultural products. Additionally, some goods and services are exempt from GST, such as healthcare services and education.

The implementation of GST has had several benefits for businesses and the economy as a whole. One of the key benefits is the simplification of the tax system, which has reduced the compliance burden on businesses and made it easier for them to conduct business across state borders. GST has also helped to reduce the cascading effect of taxes, which occurs when taxes are levied at multiple stages of production and distribution.

Another benefit of GST is the increased transparency and accountability in the tax system. The use of digital technology and the GST Network (GSTN) has made it easier for businesses to comply with the tax system and for the government to track transactions and detect tax evasion. This has helped to improve the overall efficiency and effectiveness of the tax system.

However, the implementation of GST has also faced some challenges and criticisms. One of the main criticisms is the complexity of the GST system, which has led to confusion and compliance issues for some businesses. There have also been concerns about the impact of GST on small businesses and the informal sector.

Overall, the implementation of GST has been a significant reform that has helped to simplify the tax system and reduce the compliance burden on businesses. While there have been some challenges and criticisms, GST has had a positive impact on the Indian economy and is expected to continue to play an important role in the years ahead.

The idea of a Goods and Services Tax (GST) was first proposed in India in the early 2000s. A task force was set up in 2003 to examine the feasibility of introducing GST in India, and in 2006, the then finance minister P. Chidambaram proposed the introduction of GST by 1 April 2010.

However, the implementation of GST was delayed due to concerns raised by some state governments, who were worried about losing their fiscal autonomy. The proposal for GST was revised several times over the years, with negotiations between the central government and the states continuing until 2016.

In 2014, the newly elected government led by Prime Minister Narendra Modi announced its commitment to introducing GST. A committee was set up to draft the GST law, which was introduced in Parliament in December

2014. However, the bill faced opposition from some political parties, and it was referred to a parliamentary committee for further review.

After several rounds of negotiations and revisions, the GST Bill was finally passed by the Indian Parliament on August 8, 2016. The bill was then ratified by the required number of states, and the GST Council was formed to oversee the implementation of GST.

The GST Council met several times to finalize the rules and rates for GST, and the GST Network (GSTN) was set up to enable the online registration and filing of GST returns. The government also conducted several awareness campaigns to educate businesses and consumers about the new tax system.

Finally, on July 1, 2017, GST was implemented across India, making it one of the most significant tax reforms in the country's history. The implementation of GST involved the subsuming of over a dozen indirect taxes and the creation of a single, unified tax system.

The implementation of GST was initially met with some challenges, including technical glitches in the GSTN and confusion among businesses regarding the new tax rates and compliance requirements. However, the government worked to address these issues and make the transition to GST as smooth as possible.

Overall, the implementation of GST has been a significant step towards simplifying the tax system and reducing the compliance burden on businesses. While there have been some challenges and criticisms, GST has had a positive impact on the Indian economy and is expected to continue to play an important role in the years ahead.

The Goods and Services Tax (GST) is a value-added tax on goods and services that was introduced in India in 2017. It replaced a complex web of indirect taxes that had been in place for decades, and was intended to simplify the tax system, boost compliance, and reduce the burden of compliance for businesses. In this essay, we will discuss the economic impact of GST on the Indian economy, including its effects on inflation, GDP growth, tax collections, and business operations.

Positive impact of GST:

1. Simplified tax system: GST has simplified the tax system by subsuming a number of indirect taxes, including excise duty, service tax, and value-added tax, among others. This has reduced the compliance burden on businesses, as they no longer need to keep track of multiple tax rates and

file multiple tax returns.

2. Increase in tax collections: GST has resulted in an increase in tax collections for the government. According to the Ministry of Finance, the total GST revenue collected in the financial year 2020-21 was over Rs 1.1 lakh crore per month. This has helped the government to increase its revenue base and reduce the fiscal deficit.

3. Boost to GDP growth: GST has had a positive impact on the Indian economy by boosting GDP growth. According to a study by the National Council of Applied Economic Research (NCAER), GST is estimated to have contributed to an increase in GDP growth of between 0.9 and 1.7 percentage points.

4. Reduction in prices: GST has led to a reduction in prices for many goods and services, as the tax burden has been reduced due to the elimination of cascading taxes. This has had a positive impact on consumers, as it has helped to reduce the cost of living.

Negative impact of GST:

1. Initial disruption: The implementation of GST led to some initial disruption, as businesses had to adjust to the new tax system and compliance requirements. This led to a temporary slowdown in economic activity, as businesses adjusted to the new system.

2. Increase in prices of some goods and services: While GST has led to a reduction in prices for many goods and services, it has also led to an increase in prices for some goods and services. This is because some goods and services were taxed at a lower rate under the previous tax system, and are now subject to a higher tax rate under GST.

3. Complexity of compliance: While GST has simplified the tax system in many ways, it has also introduced some complexity in terms of compliance. Businesses must now file multiple tax returns, maintain detailed records, and comply with a range of other regulations.

4. Impact on small businesses: The compliance burden of GST has had a disproportionate impact on small businesses, many of whom have struggled to adapt to the new system. This has led to some negative impact on small businesses, including closures and job losses.

Conclusion:

Overall, the implementation of GST has had a significant impact on the Indian economy, both positive and negative. While it has led to a simplified tax system, increased tax collections, and boosted GDP growth, it has also led to some initial disruption, complexity of compliance, and negative impact on small businesses. However, the long-term impact of GST is likely to be positive, as it is expected to help India to attract more investment, create jobs, and become a more competitive economy. Therefore, the government should continue to work to address the challenges posed by GST and ensure that it continues to deliver benefits to the Indian economy in the years ahead.

Demonetization refers to the process of discontinuing the legal tender status of currency notes and coins of a particular denomination. In India, demonetization refers to the decision taken by the government to discontinue the use of Rs. 500 and Rs. 1000 notes as legal tender on November 8, 2016. The decision was aimed at curbing the circulation of black money, counterfeit currency, and terror financing in the economy. In this article, we will discuss demonetization, its objectives, impact, and other relevant aspects.

Objectives of Demonetization:

The main objectives of demonetization in India were:

1. Curbing Black Money: The government of India aimed to curb the circulation of black money in the economy by demonetizing the high-value currency notes. Black money refers to the unaccounted wealth generated through illegal means such as tax evasion, corruption, and money laundering.
2. Eliminating Fake Currency: Demonetization was aimed at curbing the circulation of counterfeit currency notes in the economy. Fake currency notes are often used to finance illegal activities such as terror funding, drug trafficking, and other criminal activities.
3. Promoting Digital Transactions: Another objective of demonetization was to promote digital transactions and reduce the dependence on cash transactions. The government aimed to make the economy less cash-dependent by encouraging digital transactions.

Impact of Demonetization:

The impact of demonetization was both positive and negative. Let us look at the impact of demonetization on different sectors of the economy.

1. Impact on Black Money: The government claimed that demonetization helped in curbing black money in the economy. The Reserve Bank of India (RBI) in its annual report of 2017-18 stated that about 99.3% of the demonetized currency notes were returned to the banks. This led to a debate about the effectiveness of demonetization in curbing black money.

2. Impact on the Informal Sector: The informal sector, which is largely dependent on cash transactions, was severely impacted by demonetization. The cash crunch led to a decline in demand for goods and services, which affected the earnings of the people employed in the informal sector.

3. Impact on the Banking Sector: Demonetization led to a surge in deposits in the banking sector. Banks saw a rise in deposits as people rushed to deposit their old currency notes in the banks. However, the increase in deposits was accompanied by an increase in withdrawals, which led to a liquidity crunch in the banking sector.

4. Impact on Digital Transactions: Demonetization led to an increase in digital transactions in the economy. The government promoted the use of digital payment methods such as debit cards, credit cards, and mobile wallets to reduce the dependence on cash transactions.

5. Impact on GDP: Demonetization had a short-term negative impact on the GDP of the country. The GDP growth rate for the fiscal year 2016-17 was estimated to be 7.1%, which was lower than the previous year's growth rate of 8%.

Conclusion:

In conclusion, demonetization was a bold move by the government to curb black money, eliminate counterfeit currency, and promote digital transactions. The impact of demonetization was mixed, with both positive and negative consequences. While the government claimed that demonetization helped in curbing black money, the effectiveness of the move is still a matter of debate. Demonetization had a short-term negative impact on the GDP, but it helped in promoting digital transactions in the economy.

Tax evasion refers to the illegal act of not paying taxes owed to the government. It is a deliberate attempt by individuals, businesses, or corporations to avoid paying taxes through illegal means, such as underreporting income, hiding assets, or claiming false deductions. Tax evasion is considered a serious crime in most countries and can result in severe penalties, including fines, imprisonment, and asset forfeiture.

Tax evasion reduces the government's revenue and can have a significant impact on the overall economy. When individuals or businesses do not pay their taxes, it increases the burden on honest taxpayers and can lead to higher tax rates to compensate for the lost revenue. Additionally, tax evasion can lead to a lack of trust in the government and can undermine the legitimacy of the tax system.

Governments use various measures to prevent tax evasion, such as enforcing tax laws and regulations, increasing penalties for tax evaders, and implementing measures to increase transparency and accountability. Some countries have also implemented tax amnesty programs to encourage taxpayers to come forward and pay their taxes voluntarily.

In recent years, advances in technology and globalization have made it easier for individuals and businesses to evade taxes, leading to increased attention on this issue. Governments around the world are taking steps to address tax evasion through measures such as information exchange agreements between countries, increased international cooperation, and the use of advanced data analysis techniques to identify potential cases of tax evasion.

Overall, tax evasion is a significant problem that can have far-reaching consequences for the economy and society. It is important for individuals and businesses to fulfill their tax obligations and for governments to take strong action to prevent and address tax evasion.

Economic Indices

Economic indices refer to statistical measures that provide information about various aspects of an economy. These indices are used to assess the performance of an economy, identify trends, and inform policy decisions. Here are some of the most commonly used economic indices:

1. Gross Domestic Product (GDP): GDP is the total value of all goods and services produced within a country's borders in a specific time period, usually a year. It is considered the most important measure of economic performance and is used to compare the economic growth of different countries.
2. Consumer Price Index (CPI): CPI measures the average price of a basket of goods and services purchased by households. It is used to track inflation and is an important tool for monetary policy.
3. Unemployment rate: The unemployment rate measures the percentage of the labor force that is unemployed but actively seeking employment. It is used to assess the health of the labor market and can be an indicator of overall economic conditions.
4. Balance of trade: The balance of trade measures the difference between a country's exports and imports. It is used to assess a country's competitiveness in international trade and its reliance on imports or exports.
5. Purchasing Managers Index (PMI): PMI measures the level of activity in the manufacturing sector. It is based on surveys of purchasing managers and is used to track changes in production, new orders, and employment.
6. Stock market indices: Stock market indices such as the Dow Jones Industrial Average, S&P 500, and NASDAQ provide information about the performance of stock markets. They are used to assess the performance of companies and can provide insights into broader

economic trends.

7. Human Development Index (HDI): HDI measures a country's overall social and economic development, based on factors such as education, health, and income. It is used to assess the well-being of a population and to inform policy decisions related to social and economic development.

Overall, economic indices are important tools for understanding the performance of an economy and informing policy decisions. They provide valuable information about key economic indicators and can help policymakers identify areas for improvement and implement effective policies.

The Human Development Index (HDI) is a measure of a country's overall social and economic development, created by the United Nations Development Programme (UNDP) in 1990. The HDI combines three indicators: life expectancy, education, and income, to provide a comprehensive view of a country's human development. This index is widely used to compare the development of different countries and to track progress over time.

The HDI is based on the idea that economic growth alone is not sufficient for human development. The index recognizes the importance of social and economic factors that contribute to a high quality of life, such as education, healthcare, and access to basic needs. By focusing on these factors, the HDI provides a more holistic measure of development than traditional economic indicators like GDP.

The three components of the HDI are:

1. Life expectancy at birth: This measures the average number of years a person can expect to live at birth. This indicator is used to capture the health aspect of human development.

2. Education: This component is based on two factors: years of schooling and expected years of schooling. Years of schooling measures the average number of years of education that a person aged 25 years or older has received. Expected years of schooling measures the average number of years of education that a child of school entrance age can expect to receive if prevailing patterns of age-specific enrolment rates stay the same throughout the child's life. The education component of the HDI reflects the knowledge and skills that people possess.

3. Gross National Income (GNI) per capita: This measures the average income of a country's citizens, adjusted for purchasing power parity (PPP). This indicator is used to capture the economic aspect of human development.

The HDI is calculated on a scale from 0 to 1, with 1 being the highest possible score. Countries are then categorized into four groups based on their HDI scores: very high human development, high human development, medium human development, and low human development.

As of 2021, Norway had the highest HDI score, followed by Ireland, Switzerland, Hong Kong SAR (China), and Iceland. The lowest HDI scores were recorded in the Central African Republic, Chad, South Sudan, Niger, and Mozambique.

The HDI has been widely used to measure progress in human development over time. According to the UNDP, the global HDI value increased by 21% between 1990 and 2020, reflecting improvements in life expectancy, education, and income. However, progress has been uneven across countries and regions. While some countries have made significant gains in human development, others continue to lag behind.

The HDI has also been criticized for its limitations. Some critics argue that the index does not capture important dimensions of human development, such as political freedom and gender equality. Others argue that the HDI's focus on averages masks important inequalities within countries.

Despite these criticisms, the HDI remains an important tool for understanding the state of human development around the world. The index has helped to raise awareness about the importance of social and economic factors in promoting human well-being and has informed policies aimed at improving human development outcomes.

2021 Human Development Report:

Rank

Country

HDI Value

1

Norway

0.957

2

Switzerland
0.955
3
Ireland
0.955
4
Germany
0.947
5
Hong Kong (SAR), China
0.947
6
Australia
0.944
7
Iceland
0.944
8
Sweden
0.944
9
Singapore
0.938
10
Netherlands
0.938
11
Denmark
0.937
12
Finland
0.938
13
Canada
0.926
14
United Kingdom
0.925

15
Belgium
0.919
16
Japan
0.919
17
New Zealand
0.917
18
Austria
0.916
19
Luxembourg
0.915
20
United States of America
0.914
21
France
0.901
22
Israel
0.901
23
Slovenia
0.896
24
Spain
0.893
25
Italy
0.892
26
Czech Republic
0.891
27
Greece

0.890

28

South Korea

0.889

29

Estonia

0.885

30

Malta

0.884

31

Cyprus

0.880

32

Lithuania

0.878

33

Poland

0.876

34

Latvia

0.874

35

Slovakia

0.859

36

Chile

0.851

37

United Arab Emirates

0.848

38

Bahrain

0.846

39

Croatia

0.845

40

Uruguay
0.841
41
Saudi Arabia
0.840
42
Qatar
0.838
43
Hungary
0.837
44
Romania
0.835
45
Belarus
0.829
46
Brunei Darussalam
0.829
47
Kazakhstan
0.829
48
Palau
0.829
49
Montenegro
0.827
50
Russian Federation
0.824

PQLI stands for Physical Quality of Life Index, which is an index used to measure the quality of life of individuals or populations. The index was developed by Morris David Morris, a British economist, in 1979. The PQLI is based on three factors: basic literacy rate, infant mortality rate, and life expectancy at age one. Each of these factors is an important indicator of the overall quality of life of a population.

The basic literacy rate is the percentage of individuals in a population who are able to read and write at a basic level. This factor is important because literacy is a fundamental skill that enables individuals to access education, employment opportunities, and other resources that can improve their quality of life. A high literacy rate is generally associated with higher levels of economic development and better health outcomes.

The infant mortality rate is the number of deaths of infants under one year of age per 1,000 live births. This factor is important because it reflects the quality of healthcare and other social and environmental factors that affect the health and well-being of infants. High infant mortality rates are generally associated with poverty, inadequate healthcare, and poor living conditions.

Life expectancy at age one is the number of years a person can expect to live, on average, after reaching age one. This factor is important because it reflects the overall health and well-being of a population. High life expectancies are generally associated with good healthcare, nutrition, and living conditions.

The PQLI is calculated by taking the geometric mean of these three factors. The geometric mean is a type of average that is calculated by multiplying the values of the factors together and then taking the nth root, where n is the number of factors. For example, if the basic literacy rate is 90%, the infant mortality rate is 20 per 1,000 live births, and the life expectancy at age one is 75 years, the PQLI would be calculated as follows:

PQLI = (0.9 x 0.98 x 0.78)^(1/3) = 0.885

The PQLI ranges from 0 to 1, with higher values indicating a higher quality of life. A PQLI of 1 would indicate that all individuals in the population are literate, there are no infant deaths, and life expectancy is infinite.

The PQLI has been used to compare the quality of life of populations in different countries and regions. It has been found that countries with higher PQLI scores generally have higher levels of economic development, better healthcare systems, and higher levels of social equality. However, the PQLI has also been criticized for its limited scope, as it only includes three factors and does not account for other important indicators of quality of life, such as income, access to clean water and sanitation, and political freedom.

In conclusion, the PQLI is a useful index for measuring the quality of life of populations based on basic literacy rate, infant mortality rate, and life expectancy at age one. While it has its limitations, it can provide valuable insights into the social, economic, and environmental factors that affect the well-being of individuals and populations. By monitoring changes in PQLI scores over time, policymakers and researchers can identify areas where interventions are needed to improve the quality of life of people around the world.

Ease of Doing Business (EODB) is a measure of the regulatory environment and other factors that affect the establishment and operation of businesses in a particular country or region. The concept was developed by the World Bank Group and is based on a set of indicators that measure various aspects of the business environment, such as the ease of starting a business, obtaining permits and licenses, registering property, getting credit, paying taxes, and enforcing contracts.

The EODB rankings are published annually by the World Bank Group in the Doing Business report, which compares the business environment in 190 countries around the world. The rankings are based on a composite score that takes into account the performance of each country on ten different indicators. These indicators are:

1. Starting a business: Measures the number of procedures, time, and cost required to start a new business.
2. Dealing with construction permits: Measures the procedures, time, and cost required to obtain construction permits.
3. Getting electricity: Measures the procedures, time, and cost required to obtain a permanent electricity connection for a new building.
4. Registering property: Measures the procedures, time, and cost required to register property.
5. Getting credit: Measures the strength of credit reporting systems and the legal rights of borrowers and lenders.
6. Protecting minority investors: Measures the strength of minority shareholder protections against abusive actions by majority shareholders or company insiders.
7. Paying taxes: Measures the ease of paying taxes and the total tax rate as a percentage of profits.
8. Trading across borders: Measures the time and cost required to export and import goods.
9. Enforcing contracts: Measures the time and cost required to resolve a commercial dispute through the judicial system.

10. Resolving insolvency: Measures the time, cost, and outcome of insolvency proceedings.

The EODB rankings are designed to provide a simple, quantitative measure of the business environment in different countries, which can be useful for policymakers, businesses, and investors. Countries that perform well on the EODB rankings are generally seen as more attractive destinations for investment and business activity, as they have a more supportive regulatory environment that facilitates economic growth and development.

However, the EODB rankings have also been criticized for their narrow focus on regulatory factors, which do not capture broader issues such as infrastructure, human capital, and political stability. In addition, some experts argue that the rankings may be overly influenced by the preferences and biases of the World Bank Group and other international organizations, which may not accurately reflect the needs and priorities of local businesses and investors.

In conclusion, Ease of Doing Business is an important measure of the business environment in different countries that can provide valuable insights for policymakers, businesses, and investors. While the rankings have their limitations and criticisms, they remain a useful tool for understanding the regulatory environment and other factors that affect the establishment and operation of businesses around the world As of the latest Doing Business report published by the World Bank Group in 2020, India's ranking on the Ease of Doing Business index was 63rd out of 190 countries surveyed. India's ranking improved by 14 positions from the previous year's ranking of 77th.

India's improvement in the ranking was mainly attributed to reforms in various areas such as starting a business, dealing with construction permits, getting electricity, registering property, paying taxes, and resolving insolvency. India also implemented significant improvements in trading across borders, which included enhancements to its electronic submission system and the introduction of a single-window customs clearance system.

Despite the improvement in ranking, India still faces several challenges in creating a business-friendly environment. For example, India ranks low in enforcing contracts, which affects the ability of businesses to resolve disputes efficiently. The country also faces challenges in improving the ease of obtaining credit, which can hinder the growth of small and medium-sized enterprises.

The Indian government has continued to make efforts to improve the Ease of Doing Business in the country, with initiatives such as the introduction of the Insolvency and Bankruptcy Code, the digitization of land records, and the simplification of the tax system. The government has also set a goal of breaking into the top 50 rankings in the Ease of Doing Business index.

In conclusion, while India has made progress in improving its Ease of Doing Business ranking, there is still room for improvement. The government's efforts to reform and simplify regulations, as well as to address some of the country's infrastructure and institutional challenges, are critical to making India a more attractive destination for businesses and investors.

ifferent indicators of the Ease of Doing Business index as per the 2020 report:

Indicator

Rank

Starting a business

136

Dealing with construction permits

27

Getting electricity

22

Registering property

154

Getting credit

22

Protecting minority investors

4

Paying taxes

115

Trading across borders

68

Enforcing contracts

163

Resolving insolvency

52

Note: The rankings for each indicator are based on a scale of 0 to 100, with 0 being the worst performance and 100 being the best performance. A higher rank indicates a better performance on that indicator.

Index numbers are a statistical tool that are used to measure changes in a particular variable over time, relative to a base period. They are widely used in economics, finance, and other fields to track trends and assess the performance of different variables.

There are several types of index numbers, including price index numbers, quantity index numbers, and value index numbers. Each type of index number is used to measure changes in different variables, and they have their own specific formulas and calculations.

Price index numbers are used to measure changes in the prices of a particular set of goods or services over time. They are often used to track inflation or deflation in an economy. The formula for a simple price index number is:

Price index = (Price in current period / Price in base period) x 100

In this formula, the price in the current period is divided by the price in the base period, and the result is multiplied by 100 to convert the result into a percentage. The base period is typically chosen as a reference point, and the price index number measures the change in prices from that point forward.

Quantity index numbers are used to measure changes in the quantity of a particular good or service over time. They are often used in manufacturing and production settings to track output or productivity. The formula for a simple quantity index number is:

Quantity index = (Quantity in current period / Quantity in base period) x 100

In this formula, the quantity in the current period is divided by the quantity in the base period, and the result is multiplied by 100 to convert the result into a percentage. The base period is typically chosen as a reference point, and the quantity index number measures the change in quantity from that point forward.

Value index numbers are used to measure changes in the value of a particular variable over time. They are often used to track changes in the overall size of an economy or market. The formula for a simple value index number is:

Value index = (Value in current period / Value in base period) x 100

In this formula, the value in the current period is divided by the value in the base period, and the result is multiplied by 100 to convert the result into a percentage. The base period is typically chosen as a reference point, and the value index number measures the change in value from that point forward.

There are also different types of weighted index numbers, which are used to measure changes in a variable that is composed of several different components. For example, the consumer price index (CPI) is a weighted index number that measures changes in the price of a basket of goods and services that are typically consumed by households. The formula for a simple weighted index number is:

Weighted index = (Sum of (Weight x Value in current period) / Sum of (Weight x Value in base period)) x 100

In this formula, the weight represents the relative importance of each component of the variable being measured, and the value represents the value of each component in the current or base period. The sum of the weighted values in the current period is divided by the sum of the weighted values in the base period, and the result is multiplied by 100 to convert the result into a percentage.

In conclusion, index numbers are a useful tool for measuring changes in a particular variable over time. They allow us to track trends and assess the performance of different variables, and they have a wide range of applications in economics, finance, and other fields. The different types of index numbers each have their own specific formulas and calculations, which are used to measure changes in different variables.

The Paasche price index, also known as the current weighted index or current price index, is a type of price index that is used to measure changes in the price of a particular basket of goods and services over time. It is named after the German economist Hermann Paasche, who first proposed the index in 1874.

The Paasche price index is a weighted index, which means that it takes into account the relative importance or weighting of each item in the basket of goods and services being measured. The weights are based on the current period, which means that they reflect the current consumption patterns of the population.

To calculate the Paasche price index, we need to follow several steps:

1. Define the basket of goods and services: The first step in calculating the Paasche price index is to define the basket of goods and services that we want to measure. This could be a basket of consumer goods and services, a basket of industrial goods, or any other set of goods and services that we are interested in tracking.
2. Collect data on the prices and quantities of each item in the basket: The next step is to collect data on the prices and quantities of each item in the basket for the current period. This data can be collected through surveys, price indices, or other sources.
3. Calculate the expenditure on each item in the basket: We then need to calculate the total expenditure on each item in the basket by multiplying the price of each item by the quantity consumed.
4. Calculate the weighting of each item in the basket: We then need to calculate the weighting of each item in the basket by dividing the expenditure on each item by the total expenditure on all items in the basket.
5. Calculate the Paasche price index: The final step is to calculate the Paasche price index by dividing the current expenditure on the basket of goods and services by the base-period expenditure on the same basket, and multiplying the result by 100. The formula for the Paasche price index is:

Paasche price index = (Current expenditure on basket / Base-period expenditure on basket) x 100

The Paasche price index measures the change in the cost of purchasing the same basket of goods and services over time, taking into account the changing relative importance or weighting of each item in the basket. If the Paasche price index is greater than 100, it indicates that the cost of purchasing the basket of goods and services has increased since the base period. If it is less than 100, it indicates that the cost has decreased.

One of the advantages of the Paasche price index is that it reflects the current consumption patterns of the population, which can change over time. This means that the weights used in the index are updated to reflect these changes, making it a more accurate measure of price changes than other types of indices that use fixed weights.

However, the Paasche price index also has some limitations. One limitation is that it can be affected by changes in the quality of goods and services. If the quality of an item in the basket improves over time, its price may increase, but this does not necessarily reflect an increase in the cost of purchasing the same level of quality. Another limitation is that it can be sensitive to outliers, or extreme values, in the data, which can distort the overall index.

In conclusion, the Paasche price index is a useful tool for measuring changes in the cost of purchasing a particular basket of goods and services over time, taking into account the changing relative importance of each item in the basket. It is a weighted index that is based on current consumption patterns, which makes it a more accurate measure of price changes than other types of indices that use fixed weights. However, it also has some limitations, which need to be

The Laspeyres price index, named after the German economist Étienne Laspeyres, is a type of price index that is used to measure changes in the price of a particular basket of goods and services over time. It is also known as the base-weighted index or the fixed-weighted index.

The Laspeyres price index is a fixed-weighted index, which means that it uses a fixed set of weights to calculate the index, based on the prices and quantities of goods and services in a base period. These weights are based on the consumption patterns of the population in the base period and do not change over time.

To calculate the Laspeyres price index, we need to follow several steps:

1. Define the basket of goods and services: The first step in calculating the Laspeyres price index is to define the basket of goods and services that we want to measure. This could be a basket of consumer goods and services, a basket of industrial goods, or any other set of goods and services that we are interested in tracking.

2. Select a base period: We then need to select a base period against which we will measure the changes in the price of the basket of goods and services. The base period is typically a period in which the prices and quantities of goods and services are representative of typical consumption patterns.

3. Collect data on the prices and quantities of each item in the basket for the base period: We then need to collect data on the prices and quantities of each item in the basket for the base period. This data can be collected through surveys, price indices, or other sources.

4. Calculate the expenditure on each item in the basket in the base period: We then need to calculate the total expenditure on each item in the

basket by multiplying the price of each item by the quantity consumed in the base period.

5. Calculate the weighting of each item in the basket: We then need to calculate the weighting of each item in the basket by dividing the expenditure on each item in the base period by the total expenditure on all items in the basket in the base period.

6. Collect data on the prices and quantities of each item in the basket for the current period: We then need to collect data on the prices and quantities of each item in the basket for the current period. This data can be collected through surveys, price indices, or other sources.

7. Calculate the expenditure on each item in the basket in the current period: We then need to calculate the total expenditure on each item in the basket by multiplying the price of each item by the quantity consumed in the current period.

8. Calculate the Laspeyres price index: The final step is to calculate the Laspeyres price index by dividing the current expenditure on the basket of goods and services by the base-period expenditure on the same basket, and multiplying the result by 100. The formula for the Laspeyres price index is:

Laspeyres price index = (Current expenditure on basket / Base-period expenditure on basket) x 100

The Laspeyres price index measures the change in the cost of purchasing the same basket of goods and services over time, using fixed weights based on the consumption patterns in the base period. If the Laspeyres price index is greater than 100, it indicates that the cost of purchasing the basket of goods and services has increased since the base period. If it is less than 100, it indicates that the cost has decreased.

One of the advantages of the Laspeyres price index is that it is relatively easy to calculate and interpret. It also provides a useful baseline for comparing changes in the price of goods and services over time.

However, the Laspeyres price index also has some limitations. One limitation is that

Price indices are an important tool for measuring inflation and tracking changes in the prices of goods and services over time. They have a wide range of real-life applications, from helping policymakers make decisions about monetary and fiscal policy to informing business decisions about pricing and inventory management.

One of the most common applications of price indices is in the measurement of inflation. The consumer price index (CPI) is a widely used measure of inflation that tracks changes in the prices of a basket of goods and services consumed by households. The CPI is used by central banks, governments, and businesses to monitor inflation and make decisions about monetary and fiscal policy. If the CPI is rising too quickly, policymakers may raise interest rates or reduce government spending to slow down the economy and keep inflation under control.

Price indices are also used in the calculation of real wages, which are wages adjusted for inflation. Real wages are important because they give us a better understanding of how much purchasing power workers have. If nominal wages (wages before adjusting for inflation) are increasing, but prices are increasing even faster, then workers are effectively earning less in real terms. By calculating real wages using price indices, we can better understand changes in living standards over time.

Price indices also have important applications in the financial sector. For example, bond prices are highly sensitive to changes in inflation expectations. As inflation rises, bond prices tend to fall because investors demand higher yields to compensate for the erosion of their purchasing power. By monitoring inflation expectations using price indices, bond investors can make better-informed investment decisions.

Another application of price indices is in the pricing of goods and services. Businesses use price indices to track changes in the cost of inputs such as labor and raw materials, which can affect their pricing decisions. For example, if the cost of raw materials is increasing faster than the price of finished goods, businesses may need to raise their prices to maintain profitability. Price indices can also be used by businesses to adjust their inventory levels, as changes in prices can affect demand for different products.

Price indices are also used in international trade. The exchange rate between two countries is often affected by differences in inflation rates, as investors demand higher returns in countries with higher inflation to compensate for the loss of purchasing power. By tracking changes in inflation using price indices, businesses and investors can make more informed decisions about currency exchange and international trade.

In addition to their practical applications, price indices are also used in academic research to better understand the drivers of inflation and the effects of monetary and fiscal policy. For example, economists use price indices to estimate the relationship between changes in the money supply and changes in prices. They also use price indices to study the impact of supply shocks, such as changes in the cost of oil, on inflation.

However, price indices also have some limitations that can affect their real-life applications. One limitation is that they are based on statistical averages and may not reflect the prices that individual consumers or businesses actually pay. For example, the CPI may not accurately reflect the prices that seniors pay for healthcare or the prices that businesses pay for specialized equipment. Additionally, price indices may not reflect changes in quality over time. For example, the price of a laptop may remain constant, but the quality may improve, leading to a lower effective price. Finally, price indices may be subject to measurement errors, such as errors in sampling or data collection.

In conclusion, price indices are a critical tool for measuring inflation and tracking changes in the prices of goods and services over time. They have a wide range of real-life applications, from informing monetary and fiscal policy decisions to guiding business decisions about pricing and inventory management. While price indices have some limitations, they remain an essential tool for understanding changes in the economy and making informed decisions about investments and policy.

Rayees Ali is a well-known author, educator, vlogger, and content creator who has made a significant impact in the world of education and personal development. With over a decade of experience in teaching and learning, Rayees has become a trusted authority on a range of subjects, including economics, business, finance, and personal growth.

As an author, Rayees has written several books that aim to simplify complex concepts and make them accessible to a wider audience. His writing style is engaging and easy to understand, making his books popular among students, professionals, and enthusiasts alike. He has authored books on various topics, including economics, entrepreneurship, investing, and personal finance.

As an educator, Rayees has a passion for teaching and sharing knowledge with others. He has taught in various academic institutions and has also developed online courses that have helped thousands of learners worldwide. He believes in the power of education to transform lives and help individuals reach their full potential.

As a vlogger and content creator, Rayees has a strong online presence, with a large following on social media platforms such as YouTube and

Instagram. He uses these platforms to share his knowledge and expertise with a wider audience, and his videos and posts are informative, engaging, and often thought-provoking.

Rayees is also a strong advocate for personal growth and development, and he believes that anyone can achieve success with the right mindset and approach. He often shares his insights and tips for personal growth and success, helping individuals to develop their skills, improve their mindset, and achieve their goals.

In conclusion, Rayees Ali is a multi-talented individual who has made a significant impact in the worlds of education and personal development. His books, teaching, and online content have helped countless individuals to learn, grow, and achieve their goals. With his passion for knowledge and his commitment to making learning accessible to all, Rayees is an inspiration to many and a valuable resource for anyone looking to expand their knowledge and skills.

I dedicate my work to my parents and Aman with deep gratitude and love. My parents have been a constant source of support and inspiration throughout my life. They have always encouraged me to pursue my dreams and have provided me with the tools and opportunities to succeed. Their unwavering love and belief in me have been instrumental in shaping who I am today.

I also dedicate this work to Aman, who has been a close friend and mentor. Aman's guidance and support have been invaluable to me throughout my academic and professional journey. His unwavering commitment to excellence and his dedication to helping others have inspired me to strive for the same.

I am deeply grateful to my parents and Aman for their unwavering love, support, and guidance. Their presence in my life has made all the difference, and I am honored to dedicate this work to them.

Chapter : 09

Various economic indices :

Economic indices refer to statistical measures that provide information about various aspects of an economy. These indices are used to assess the performance of an economy, identify trends, and inform policy decisions. Here are some of the most commonly used economic indices:

1. Gross Domestic Product (GDP): GDP is the total value of all goods and services produced within a country's borders in a specific time period,

usually a year. It is considered the most important measure of economic performance and is used to compare the economic growth of different countries.

2. Consumer Price Index (CPI): CPI measures the average price of a basket of goods and services purchased by households. It is used to track inflation and is an important tool for monetary policy.

3. Unemployment rate: The unemployment rate measures the percentage of the labor force that is unemployed but actively seeking employment. It is used to assess the health of the labor market and can be an indicator of overall economic conditions.

4. Balance of trade: The balance of trade measures the difference between a country's exports and imports. It is used to assess a country's competitiveness in international trade and its reliance on imports or exports.

5. Purchasing Managers Index (PMI): PMI measures the level of activity in the manufacturing sector. It is based on surveys of purchasing managers and is used to track changes in production, new orders, and employment.

6. Stock market indices: Stock market indices such as the Dow Jones Industrial Average, S&P 500, and NASDAQ provide information about the performance of stock markets. They are used to assess the performance of companies and can provide insights into broader economic trends.

7. Human Development Index (HDI): HDI measures a country's overall social and economic development, based on factors such as education, health, and income. It is used to assess the well-being of a population and to inform policy decisions related to social and economic development.

Overall, economic indices are important tools for understanding the performance of an economy and informing policy decisions. They provide valuable information about key economic indicators and can help policymakers identify areas for improvement and implement effective policies.

The Human Development Index (HDI) is a measure of a country's overall social and economic development, created by the United Nations Development Programme (UNDP) in 1990. The HDI combines three indicators: life expectancy, education, and income, to provide a comprehensive view of a country's human development. This index is widely used to compare the development of different countries and to track progress over time.

The HDI is based on the idea that economic growth alone is not sufficient for human development. The index recognizes the importance of social and economic factors that contribute to a high quality of life, such as education, healthcare, and access to basic needs. By focusing on these factors, the HDI provides a more holistic measure of development than traditional economic indicators like GDP.

The three components of the HDI are:

1. Life expectancy at birth: This measures the average number of years a person can expect to live at birth. This indicator is used to capture the health aspect of human development.
2. Education: This component is based on two factors: years of schooling and expected years of schooling. Years of schooling measures the average number of years of education that a person aged 25 years or older has received. Expected years of schooling measures the average number of years of education that a child of school entrance age can expect to receive if prevailing patterns of age-specific enrolment rates stay the same throughout the child's life. The education component of the HDI reflects the knowledge and skills that people possess.
3. Gross National Income (GNI) per capita: This measures the average income of a country's citizens, adjusted for purchasing power parity (PPP). This indicator is used to capture the economic aspect of human development.

The HDI is calculated on a scale from 0 to 1, with 1 being the highest possible score. Countries are then categorized into four groups based on their HDI scores: very high human development, high human development, medium human development, and low human development.

As of 2021, Norway had the highest HDI score, followed by Ireland, Switzerland, Hong Kong SAR (China), and Iceland. The lowest HDI scores were recorded in the Central African Republic, Chad, South Sudan, Niger, and Mozambique.

The HDI has been widely used to measure progress in human development over time. According to the UNDP, the global HDI value increased by 21% between 1990 and 2020, reflecting improvements in life expectancy, education, and income. However, progress has been uneven across countries and regions. While some countries have made significant gains in human development, others continue to lag behind.

The HDI has also been criticized for its limitations. Some critics argue that the index does not capture important dimensions of human development, such as political freedom and gender equality. Others argue that the HDI's focus on averages masks important inequalities within countries.

Despite these criticisms, the HDI remains an important tool for understanding the state of human development around the world. The index has helped to raise awareness about the importance of social and economic factors in promoting human well-being and has informed policies aimed at improving human development outcomes.

2021 Human Development Report:

Rank

Country

HDI Value

1

Norway

0.957

2

Switzerland

0.955

3

Ireland

0.955

4

Germany

0.947

5

Hong Kong (SAR), China

0.947

6

Australia

0.944

7

Iceland

0.944

8

Sweden
0.944
9
Singapore
0.938
10
Netherlands
0.938
11
Denmark
0.937
12
Finland
0.938
13
Canada
0.926
14
United Kingdom
0.925
15
Belgium
0.919
16
Japan
0.919
17
New Zealand
0.917
18
Austria
0.916
19
Luxembourg
0.915
20
United States of America
0.914

21
France
0.901
22
Israel
0.901
23
Slovenia
0.896
24
Spain
0.893
25
Italy
0.892
26
Czech Republic
0.891
27
Greece
0.890
28
South Korea
0.889
29
Estonia
0.885
30
Malta
0.884
31
Cyprus
0.880
32
Lithuania
0.878
33
Poland

0.876
34
Latvia
0.874
35
Slovakia
0.859
36
Chile
0.851
37
United Arab Emirates
0.848
38
Bahrain
0.846
39
Croatia
0.845
40
Uruguay
0.841
41
Saudi Arabia
0.840
42
Qatar
0.838
43
Hungary
0.837
44
Romania
0.835
45
Belarus
0.829
46

Brunei Darussalam

0.829

47

Kazakhstan

0.829

48

Palau

0.829

49

Montenegro

0.827

50

Russian Federation

0.824

PQLI stands for Physical Quality of Life Index, which is an index used to measure the quality of life of individuals or populations. The index was developed by Morris David Morris, a British economist, in 1979. The PQLI is based on three factors: basic literacy rate, infant mortality rate, and life expectancy at age one. Each of these factors is an important indicator of the overall quality of life of a population.

The basic literacy rate is the percentage of individuals in a population who are able to read and write at a basic level. This factor is important because literacy is a fundamental skill that enables individuals to access education, employment opportunities, and other resources that can improve their quality of life. A high literacy rate is generally associated with higher levels of economic development and better health outcomes.

The infant mortality rate is the number of deaths of infants under one year of age per 1,000 live births. This factor is important because it reflects the quality of healthcare and other social and environmental factors that affect the health and well-being of infants. High infant mortality rates are generally associated with poverty, inadequate healthcare, and poor living conditions.

Life expectancy at age one is the number of years a person can expect to live, on average, after reaching age one. This factor is important because it reflects the overall health and well-being of a population. High life expectancies are generally associated with good healthcare, nutrition, and living conditions.

The PQLI is calculated by taking the geometric mean of these three factors. The geometric mean is a type of average that is calculated by multiplying the values of the factors together and then taking the nth root, where n is the number of factors. For example, if the basic literacy rate is 90%, the infant mortality rate is 20 per 1,000 live births, and the life expectancy at age one is 75 years, the PQLI would be calculated as follows:

PQLI = (0.9 x 0.98 x 0.78)^(1/3) = 0.885

The PQLI ranges from 0 to 1, with higher values indicating a higher quality of life. A PQLI of 1 would indicate that all individuals in the population are literate, there are no infant deaths, and life expectancy is infinite.

The PQLI has been used to compare the quality of life of populations in different countries and regions. It has been found that countries with higher PQLI scores generally have higher levels of economic development, better healthcare systems, and higher levels of social equality. However, the PQLI has also been criticized for its limited scope, as it only includes three factors and does not account for other important indicators of quality of life, such as income, access to clean water and sanitation, and political freedom.

In conclusion, the PQLI is a useful index for measuring the quality of life of populations based on basic literacy rate, infant mortality rate, and life expectancy at age one. While it has its limitations, it can provide valuable insights into the social, economic, and environmental factors that affect the well-being of individuals and populations. By monitoring changes in PQLI scores over time, policymakers and researchers can identify areas where interventions are needed to improve the quality of life of people around the world.

Ease of Doing Business (EODB) is a measure of the regulatory environment and other factors that affect the establishment and operation of businesses in a particular country or region. The concept was developed by the World Bank Group and is based on a set of indicators that measure various aspects of the business environment, such as the ease of starting a business, obtaining permits and licenses, registering property, getting credit, paying taxes, and enforcing contracts.

The EODB rankings are published annually by the World Bank Group in the Doing Business report, which compares the business environment in 190 countries around the world. The rankings are based on a composite score that takes into account the performance of each country on ten different indicators. These indicators are:

1. Starting a business: Measures the number of procedures, time, and cost required to start a new business.
2. Dealing with construction permits: Measures the procedures, time, and cost required to obtain construction permits.
3. Getting electricity: Measures the procedures, time, and cost required to obtain a permanent electricity connection for a new building.
4. Registering property: Measures the procedures, time, and cost required to register property.
5. Getting credit: Measures the strength of credit reporting systems and the legal rights of borrowers and lenders.
6. Protecting minority investors: Measures the strength of minority shareholder protections against abusive actions by majority shareholders or company insiders.
7. Paying taxes: Measures the ease of paying taxes and the total tax rate as a percentage of profits.
8. Trading across borders: Measures the time and cost required to export and import goods.
9. Enforcing contracts: Measures the time and cost required to resolve a commercial dispute through the judicial system.
10. Resolving insolvency: Measures the time, cost, and outcome of insolvency proceedings.

The EODB rankings are designed to provide a simple, quantitative measure of the business environment in different countries, which can be useful for policymakers, businesses, and investors. Countries that perform well on the EODB rankings are generally seen as more attractive destinations for investment and business activity, as they have a more supportive regulatory environment that facilitates economic growth and development.

However, the EODB rankings have also been criticized for their narrow focus on regulatory factors, which do not capture broader issues such as infrastructure, human capital, and political stability. In addition, some experts argue that the rankings may be overly influenced by the preferences and biases of the World Bank Group and other international organizations, which may not accurately reflect the needs and priorities of local businesses and investors.

In conclusion, Ease of Doing Business is an important measure of the business environment in different countries that can provide valuable insights for policymakers, businesses, and investors. While the rankings have their limitations and criticisms, they remain a useful tool for understanding the regulatory environment and other factors that affect the establishment and operation of businesses around the world As of the latest Doing Business report published by the World Bank Group in 2020, India's ranking on the Ease of Doing Business index was 63rd out of 190 countries surveyed. India's ranking improved by 14 positions from the previous year's ranking of 77th.

India's improvement in the ranking was mainly attributed to reforms in various areas such as starting a business, dealing with construction permits, getting electricity, registering property, paying taxes, and resolving insolvency. India also implemented significant improvements in trading across borders, which included enhancements to its electronic submission system and the introduction of a single-window customs clearance system.

Despite the improvement in ranking, India still faces several challenges in creating a business-friendly environment. For example, India ranks low in enforcing contracts, which affects the ability of businesses to resolve disputes efficiently. The country also faces challenges in improving the ease of obtaining credit, which can hinder the growth of small and medium-sized enterprises.

The Indian government has continued to make efforts to improve the Ease of Doing Business in the country, with initiatives such as the introduction of the Insolvency and Bankruptcy Code, the digitization of land records, and the simplification of the tax system. The government has also set a goal of breaking into the top 50 rankings in the Ease of Doing Business index.

In conclusion, while India has made progress in improving its Ease of Doing Business ranking, there is still room for improvement. The government's efforts to reform and simplify regulations, as well as to address some of the country's infrastructure and institutional challenges, are critical to making India a more attractive destination for businesses and investors.

ifferent indicators of the Ease of Doing Business index as per the 2020 report:

Indicator

Rank

Starting a business

136

Dealing with construction permits

27

Getting electricity

22

Registering property

154

Getting credit

22

Protecting minority investors

4

Paying taxes

115

Trading across borders

68

Enforcing contracts

163

Resolving insolvency

52

Note: The rankings for each indicator are based on a scale of 0 to 100, with 0 being the worst performance and 100 being the best performance. A higher rank indicates a better performance on that indicator.

Index numbers are a statistical tool that are used to measure changes in a particular variable over time, relative to a base period. They are widely used in economics, finance, and other fields to track trends and assess the performance of different variables.

There are several types of index numbers, including price index numbers, quantity index numbers, and value index numbers. Each type of index number is used to measure changes in different variables, and they have their own specific formulas and calculations.

Price index numbers are used to measure changes in the prices of a particular set of goods or services over time. They are often used to track inflation or deflation in an economy. The formula for a simple price index number is:

Price index = (Price in current period / Price in base period) x 100

In this formula, the price in the current period is divided by the price in the base period, and the result is multiplied by 100 to convert the result into a percentage. The base period is typically chosen as a reference point, and the price index number measures the change in prices from that point forward.

Quantity index numbers are used to measure changes in the quantity of a particular good or service over time. They are often used in manufacturing and production settings to track output or productivity. The formula for a simple quantity index number is:

Quantity index = (Quantity in current period / Quantity in base period) x 100

In this formula, the quantity in the current period is divided by the quantity in the base period, and the result is multiplied by 100 to convert the result into a percentage. The base period is typically chosen as a reference point, and the quantity index number measures the change in quantity from that point forward.

Value index numbers are used to measure changes in the value of a particular variable over time. They are often used to track changes in the overall size of an economy or market. The formula for a simple value index number is:

Value index = (Value in current period / Value in base period) x 100

In this formula, the value in the current period is divided by the value in the base period, and the result is multiplied by 100 to convert the result into a percentage. The base period is typically chosen as a reference point, and the value index number measures the change in value from that point forward.

There are also different types of weighted index numbers, which are used to measure changes in a variable that is composed of several different components. For example, the consumer price index (CPI) is a weighted index number that measures changes in the price of a basket of goods and services that are typically consumed by households. The formula for a simple weighted index number is:

Weighted index = (Sum of (Weight x Value in current period) / Sum of (Weight x Value in base period)) x 100

In this formula, the weight represents the relative importance of each component of the variable being measured, and the value represents the value of each component in the current or base period. The sum of the weighted values in the current period is divided by the sum of the weighted values in the base period, and the result is multiplied by 100 to convert the result into a percentage.

In conclusion, index numbers are a useful tool for measuring changes in a particular variable over time. They allow us to track trends and assess the performance of different variables, and they have a wide range of applications in economics, finance, and other fields. The different types of index numbers each have their own specific formulas and calculations, which are used to measure changes in different variables.

The Paasche price index, also known as the current weighted index or current price index, is a type of price index that is used to measure changes in the price of a particular basket of goods and services over time. It is named after the German economist Hermann Paasche, who first proposed the index in 1874.

The Paasche price index is a weighted index, which means that it takes into account the relative importance or weighting of each item in the basket of goods and services being measured. The weights are based on the current period, which means that they reflect the current consumption patterns of the population.

To calculate the Paasche price index, we need to follow several steps:

1. Define the basket of goods and services: The first step in calculating the Paasche price index is to define the basket of goods and services that we want to measure. This could be a basket of consumer goods and services, a basket of industrial goods, or any other set of goods and services that we are interested in tracking.
2. Collect data on the prices and quantities of each item in the basket: The next step is to collect data on the prices and quantities of each item in the basket for the current period. This data can be collected through surveys, price indices, or other sources.
3. Calculate the expenditure on each item in the basket: We then need to calculate the total expenditure on each item in the basket by multiplying the price of each item by the quantity consumed.
4. Calculate the weighting of each item in the basket: We then need to calculate the weighting of each item in the basket by dividing the expenditure on each item by the total expenditure on all items in the basket.
5. Calculate the Paasche price index: The final step is to calculate the Paasche price index by dividing the current expenditure on the basket of goods and services by the base-period expenditure on the same basket, and multiplying the result by 100. The formula for the Paasche price index is:

Paasche price index = (Current expenditure on basket / Base-period expenditure on basket) x 100

The Paasche price index measures the change in the cost of purchasing the same basket of goods and services over time, taking into account the changing relative importance or weighting of each item in the basket. If the Paasche price index is greater than 100, it indicates that the cost of purchasing the basket of goods and services has increased since the base period. If it is less than 100, it indicates that the cost has decreased.

One of the advantages of the Paasche price index is that it reflects the current consumption patterns of the population, which can change over time. This means that the weights used in the index are updated to reflect these changes, making it a more accurate measure of price changes than other types of indices that use fixed weights.

However, the Paasche price index also has some limitations. One limitation is that it can be affected by changes in the quality of goods and services. If the quality of an item in the basket improves over time, its price may increase, but this does not necessarily reflect an increase in the cost of purchasing the same level of quality. Another limitation is that it can be sensitive to outliers, or extreme values, in the data, which can distort the overall index.

In conclusion, the Paasche price index is a useful tool for measuring changes in the cost of purchasing a particular basket of goods and services over time, taking into account the changing relative importance of each item in the basket. It is a weighted index that is based on current consumption patterns, which makes it a more accurate measure of price changes than other types of indices that use fixed weights. However, it also has some limitations, which need to be

The Laspeyres price index, named after the German economist Étienne Laspeyres, is a type of price index that is used to measure changes in the price of a particular basket of goods and services over time. It is also known as the base-weighted index or the fixed-weighted index.

The Laspeyres price index is a fixed-weighted index, which means that it uses a fixed set of weights to calculate the index, based on the prices and quantities of goods and services in a base period. These weights are based on the consumption patterns of the population in the base period and do not change over time.

To calculate the Laspeyres price index, we need to follow several steps:

1. Define the basket of goods and services: The first step in calculating the Laspeyres price index is to define the basket of goods and services that we want to measure. This could be a basket of consumer goods and services, a basket of industrial goods, or any other set of goods and services that we are interested in tracking.

2. Select a base period: We then need to select a base period against which we will measure the changes in the price of the basket of goods and services. The base period is typically a period in which the prices and quantities of goods and services are representative of typical consumption patterns.

3. Collect data on the prices and quantities of each item in the basket for the base period: We then need to collect data on the prices and quantities of each item in the basket for the base period. This data can be collected through surveys, price indices, or other sources.

4. Calculate the expenditure on each item in the basket in the base period: We then need to calculate the total expenditure on each item in the basket by multiplying the price of each item by the quantity consumed in the base period.

5. Calculate the weighting of each item in the basket: We then need to calculate the weighting of each item in the basket by dividing the expenditure on each item in the base period by the total expenditure on all items in the basket in the base period.

6. Collect data on the prices and quantities of each item in the basket for the current period: We then need to collect data on the prices and quantities of each item in the basket for the current period. This data can be collected through surveys, price indices, or other sources.

7. Calculate the expenditure on each item in the basket in the current period: We then need to calculate the total expenditure on each item in the basket by multiplying the price of each item by the quantity consumed in the current period.

8. Calculate the Laspeyres price index: The final step is to calculate the Laspeyres price index by dividing the current expenditure on the basket of goods and services by the base-period expenditure on the same basket, and multiplying the result by 100. The formula for the Laspeyres price index is:

Laspeyres price index = (Current expenditure on basket / Base-period expenditure on basket) x 100

The Laspeyres price index measures the change in the cost of purchasing the same basket of goods and services over time, using fixed weights based on the consumption patterns in the base period. If the Laspeyres price index is greater than 100, it indicates that the cost of purchasing the basket of goods and services has increased since the base period. If it is less than 100, it indicates that the cost has decreased.

One of the advantages of the Laspeyres price index is that it is relatively easy to calculate and interpret. It also provides a useful baseline for comparing changes in the price of goods and services over time.

However, the Laspeyres price index also has some limitations. One limitation is that

Price indices are an important tool for measuring inflation and tracking changes in the prices of goods and services over time. They have a wide range of real-life applications, from helping policymakers make decisions about monetary and fiscal policy to informing business decisions about pricing and inventory management.

One of the most common applications of price indices is in the measurement of inflation. The consumer price index (CPI) is a widely used measure of inflation that tracks changes in the prices of a basket of goods and services consumed by households. The CPI is used by central banks, governments, and businesses to monitor inflation and make decisions about monetary and fiscal policy. If the CPI is rising too quickly, policymakers may raise interest rates or reduce government spending to slow down the economy and keep inflation under control.

Price indices are also used in the calculation of real wages, which are wages adjusted for inflation. Real wages are important because they give us a better understanding of how much purchasing power workers have. If nominal wages (wages before adjusting for inflation) are increasing, but prices are increasing even faster, then workers are effectively earning less in real terms. By calculating real wages using price indices, we can better understand changes in living standards over time.

Price indices also have important applications in the financial sector. For example, bond prices are highly sensitive to changes in inflation expectations. As inflation rises, bond prices tend to fall because investors demand higher yields to compensate for the erosion of their purchasing power. By monitoring inflation expectations using price indices, bond investors can make better-informed investment decisions.

Another application of price indices is in the pricing of goods and services. Businesses use price indices to track changes in the cost of inputs such as labor and raw materials, which can affect their pricing decisions. For example, if the cost of raw materials is increasing faster than the price of finished goods, businesses may need to raise their prices to maintain profitability. Price indices can also be used by businesses to adjust their inventory levels, as changes in prices can affect demand for different products.

Price indices are also used in international trade. The exchange rate between two countries is often affected by differences in inflation rates, as investors demand higher returns in countries with higher inflation to compensate for the loss of purchasing power. By tracking changes in inflation using price indices, businesses and investors can make more informed decisions about currency exchange and international trade.

In addition to their practical applications, price indices are also used in academic research to better understand the drivers of inflation and the effects of monetary and fiscal policy. For example, economists use price indices to estimate the relationship between changes in the money supply and changes in prices. They also use price indices to study the impact of supply shocks, such as changes in the cost of oil, on inflation.

However, price indices also have some limitations that can affect their real-life applications. One limitation is that they are based on statistical averages and may not reflect the prices that individual consumers or businesses actually pay. For example, the CPI may not accurately reflect the prices that seniors pay for healthcare or the prices that businesses pay for specialized equipment. Additionally, price indices may not reflect changes in quality over time. For example, the price of a laptop may remain constant, but the quality may improve, leading to a lower effective price. Finally, price indices may be subject to measurement errors, such as errors in sampling or data collection.

In conclusion, price indices are a critical tool for measuring inflation and tracking changes in the prices of goods and services over time. They have a wide range of real-life applications, from informing monetary and fiscal policy decisions to guiding business decisions about pricing and inventory management. While price indices have some limitations, they remain an essential tool for understanding changes in the economy and making informed decisions about investments and policy.